JOINING
The United States Army

JOINING THE MILITARY

A McFarland Handbook Series
by Snow Wildsmith

1. *Joining the United States Air Force.* 2012
2. *Joining the United States Army.* 2012
3. *Joining the United States Coast Guard.* 2012
4. *Joining the United States Marine Corps.* 2012
5. *Joining the United States Navy.* 2012

Joining the United States Army

A Handbook

SNOW WILDSMITH

JOINING THE MILITARY, 2

McFarland & Company, Inc., Publishers

Jefferson, North Carolina, and London

LIBRARY OF CONGRESS CATALOGUING-IN-PUBLICATION DATA

Wildsmith, Snow, 1973–
Joining the United States Army : a handbook / Snow Wildsmith.
p.   cm. — (Joining the military ; 2)
Includes bibliographical references and index.

ISBN 978-0-7864-4759-6
softcover : acid free paper ∞

1. United States — Army — Vocational guidance.   I. Title.
UB147.W53 2012   355.0024'73 — dc23   2012009352

BRITISH LIBRARY CATALOGUING DATA ARE AVAILABLE

On the cover: *inset* United States Army Seal; *photograph*
Major General Robert "Abe" Abrams, Third Infantry Division
commanding general, reenlists 3rd Inf. Div. Soldiers and their Families
at Fort Stewart, 2011 (Sgt. Uriah Walker, 3rd ID Public Affairs)

Manufactured in the United States of America

*McFarland & Company, Inc., Publishers
Box 611, Jefferson, North Carolina 28640
www.mcfarlandpub.com*

Joining the United States Army

A Handbook

SNOW WILDSMITH

JOINING THE MILITARY, 2

McFarland & Company, Inc., Publishers

Jefferson, North Carolina, and London

LIBRARY OF CONGRESS CATALOGUING-IN-PUBLICATION DATA

Wildsmith, Snow, 1973–
Joining the United States Army : a handbook / Snow Wildsmith.
p.   cm. — (Joining the military ; 2)
Includes bibliographical references and index.

ISBN 978-0-7864-4759-6
softcover : acid free paper ∞

1. United States — Army — Vocational guidance.   I. Title.
UB147.W53 2012   355.0024'73 — dc23   2012009352

BRITISH LIBRARY CATALOGUING DATA ARE AVAILABLE

On the cover: *inset* United States Army Seal; *photograph*
Major General Robert "Abe" Abrams, Third Infantry Division
commanding general, reenlists 3rd Inf. Div. Soldiers and their Families
at Fort Stewart, 2011 (Sgt. Uriah Walker, 3rd ID Public Affairs)

Manufactured in the United States of America

*McFarland & Company, Inc., Publishers
Box 611, Jefferson, North Carolina 28640
www.mcfarlandpub.com*

For my father,
HMCM Donald P. Wildsmith, USN (Ret.),
with love and respect for all he has given
for me and for his country.

Acknowledgments

This book could not have been written without the support of the United States Army. Thank you to all of the soldiers and civilian employees who took the time out of their busy days to answer my questions, supply me with needed information, tour me around recruit training, and generally help me out with whatever I needed.

Thank you also to librarian and friend Emily Leachman for proofreading my rough drafts and making suggestions for improvement. I owe a debt of gratitude to all of my friends and family who supported me during the writing process, especially to my ever-patient and ever-loving husband Barry.

Table of Contents

TABLE OF CONTENTS

Read This First

Patriotism. Money for college. Family tradition. Job training. Adventure. Secure employment. Travel. Service to others. The opportunity to do something different. There are as many reasons to join the military as there are people in the military. Some people want to make a full career out of their military service. Some just want to get in, do their time, and get the benefits they've earned. Others are in the middle — they aren't sure where they want to go after the military or how long they want to spend in the service, but they think it might be a good job for the time being.

Whether you are certain that you want to enter the military or you are just curious and want more information, you still will need to consider a lot of factors before you join. This series of books is designed to help you look at all of your options to see whether or not military service is right for you and, if so, to help you figure out which branch of the service is for you. There is one book for each branch of the service: Air Force, Army, Coast Guard, Marine Corps, and Navy. Within each book, there are sections on:

- Looking at your personality to see if you will fit the military lifestyle
- Talking with a recruiter to find out what the service offers and what they expect from you in return
- How enlisting works and what you need to do during the process
- Taking the Armed Services Vocational Aptitude Battery test
- Preparing for recruit training (also called basic training) mentally, physically, emotionally, and socially

- What happens during basic training
- Books, DVDs, and websites with more information on joining the military, military history, and life in the military

Joining the military is a major lifestyle change, one which will affect not only you, but also your family and your friends. You'll need to think long and hard about all of your options and the choice you are about to make. These books will give you the basic information you need, but you should know that every individual's enlistment and training experience is different, shaped by their personality, education, goals, and interests. Additionally, the branches of the military are constantly evaluating and adjusting their policies and procedures to meet their current needs. The military personnel you speak with during your time considering military service will have up-to-date information about enlistment and training.

Whatever branch you choose to serve in, however long your term of enlistment, whichever occupational specialty you pick — you will be part of something larger than you. Deciding to become a serviceman or servicewoman can be the best thing that ever happened to you as it guides the rest of your life in ways you never expected.

ONE

Thinking About Joining the Military

Things to Consider for Potential Enlistees

There are many big decisions people make over their lifetime. "Should I go to college or get a job?" "Who will I marry?" "Will I have children?" "Where will I live?" Deciding to join the military is one of those momentous decisions. If you decide to join, you will be committing yourself to service to the government for at least eight years—the length of your active duty contract plus the years you are obligated to spend in the Individual Ready Reserve, where you aren't actively doing military training and work, but can still be called up by the government. Because you will be making a legal, binding contract that cannot be gotten out of easily, you must consider all of the factors carefully before deciding to enlist in the military. Take your time, do your research, and, most of all, don't let anyone pressure you to join or not to join. This is your life and the decision should be yours.

Pros and Cons

The first thing to consider are the positives and negatives of joining the military—the pros and cons. What will you gain by joining and what will you have to sacrifice?

PROS

- Employment—joining the military will give you a job with a steady, guaranteed income as well as health insurance, housing, and a clothing allowance

- Training — the military offers training on a wide variety of jobs, and you will be paid, fed, clothed, and housed while you are training
- Education — in addition to the job training offered by the military, you will also earn money to help pay for future education; you can even start college and earn a degree while serving in the military — sometimes completely paid for by the military
- Travel — service in the military pretty much guarantees travel, both in the U.S. and around the world
- Purpose — military service is just that: service; you will be serving your country and working for something bigger than just you

CONS

- War — the first and most important job of the military is to protect the United States; by joining you face the very real possibility of ending up in a war zone
- Freedom — by joining the military you will be voluntarily giving up a good amount of your personal freedom for the regimen of military life
- Time — serving in the military means a lot of hard work, often including long hours and even days, weeks, or months away from friends and family
- Training and Education — there are a lot of training and education opportunities in the military, but the military's interest is to train you in what they need to you do, so your education desires come second if they don't fit with current military needs
- Travel — you will travel and you will have some say in where you travel to, but not always; if some get to serve in Paris or Hawaii, many serve in much less glamorous locales

These are some of the major factors to consider as you begin to think about possible military service. As you learn more about the military, you'll also need to consider whether or not you are a good candidate for the military and whether or not the military can help you achieve the goals you have set for your life.

Your Personality, Your Goals, and Your Future Aspirations

The military has its own goals and its own direction for the future and so should you. It is important that you think about what your goals are before deciding if military service is right for you. If you don't have goals planned out, now is the time to make them. Start thinking about what you might want to accomplish in the future. The military will be happy to use your hard work to accomplish its goals, but if its goals are not the same as what you want to do with your life, then your time of service will be one of frustration.

Additionally, you should think about the military lifestyle and whether or not it fits with your personality. The military is regimented, ordered, and focused on teamwork. If you are a rugged individualist, then military service might not be an easy job for you as your superiors will try to change that mindset.

This book and the others in this series focus on enlisted careers in the military. "Enlisted" means those servicemen and women who are not officers. Enlisted personnel are responsible for the daily operations of the military, whereas officers are the command personnel, the ones who give the orders. That doesn't mean that enlisted service members don't lead. There are a lot of opportunities for enlisted men and women to learn and practice leadership skills, starting as early as basic training. The higher ranks of enlisted personnel are called "non-commissioned officers" and they take on many of the leadership roles in the military. You do not need a college degree to enlist in the military, but you do need one to be commissioned — meaning appointed — as an officer. That is another factor to keep in mind as you are deciding if a military career is right for you.

MILITARY QUESTIONNAIRE

The following questionnaire will help you think about your lifestyle, your personality, and your future to see if they might fit well with the military.

Read each statement and see if "yes"—it does agree with you, "no"—it does not agree with you, or "maybe"—it sort of agrees with you or you aren't sure. There are no right or wrong answers. These are just factors to consider. The notes after each statement will help you see how that statement does or does not fit with a possible career in the military.

YES   NO   MAYBE   I am interested in serving in the military because of patriotic reasons.
- This is a great reason to join the military. Having a high degree of patriotism means that you'd be willing to offer up your life to protect and serve your country. But there are other ways that patriotic people can serve the United States, so if you aren't certain that military service is for you, consider non-military service options.

YES   NO   MAYBE   I am interested in serving in the military because I want to give back to others.
- Also a good reason to join the military, but again, if you are positive that you wish to serve others, but uncertain about the military, there are other options that will allow you to help out.

YES   NO   MAYBE   I am interested in serving in the military because my father/mother/other family member served.
- This is another good reason for joining. If you were raised in a military family or if you grew up hearing stories about a family member's military service, then you will probably be proud to serve and carry on a family tradition. Make sure, though, that you get the most recent information on military life and make sure that your personality and goals are as compatible with military service as your family member's were. Also be sure that you are not joining because....

YES   NO   MAYBE My father/mother/other family member says that I have to join the military.
- DO NOT allow yourself to be forced or coerced into military

A daughter administers the Oath as her father becomes a warrant officer in the Army (Official U.S. Army photograph by Sgt. Mary S. Katzenberger).

service. It is your life and your decision. No one else can make it for you.

YES NO MAYBE I want to serve in the military, but only part-time, and/or I don't want to have to move away from where I am living.

- Then you will want to consider enlisting as a reservist. Service men and women in the reserves serve one weekend a month and two weeks out of the year, during which time they train with a local unit. Reservists are still members of the military and are subject to the same regulations and laws as active-duty service members, as well as receiving many of the same benefits that active-duty personnel receive. You should know, however, that as a reservist you can be called up to active duty for a period of time ranging from several weeks to several years in order to fight in war. And job choices in the reserves can be limited, as they are almost always assigned based on the needs of the reserve unit with which you will serve.

YES NO MAYBE I want to serve in the military, but only for my initial term of enlistment (usually four years).
- It is possible to sign up for a four year stint in the military, complete your time, and then choose not to reenlist. However, there are some factors to keep in mind. First of all, even after you finish your term and leave the military, you are still part of the military until you have completed a full eight years of service. The enlistment contract that you sign when you join the military makes it clear that you are obligated for those eight years and that any time you don't spend as active duty must be spent in the inactive reserves, called the Individual Ready Reserve (IRR). While you are in the IRR, you can still be called up to duty if the military needs you.
- If the military still needs your services at the end of your enlistment term, it can prevent you from leaving. A program called "Stop Loss" allows the military, during times of conflict, to prevent you for up to one year from leaving at your normal separation date. The military has been using this program during the conflicts in Iraq and Afghanistan to ensure that personnel who are doing specific jobs are still around to do those jobs when the military needs them.

YES NO MAYBE I have dropped out of or not finished high school or I have my GED or I am considering dropping out of high school.
- Today's military wants service members who have at least finished high school. If you are still in school, you will need to finish and graduate, trying for the best grades you can get. If you have dropped out, you will have to get a GED in order to be eligible to enlist. However, every branch of the military has strict limitations on how many people they will accept with

GEDs each year and those candidates must score higher grades on the Armed Services Vocational Aptitude Battery (ASVAB) test which all potential enlistees must take. (More on the ASVAB in Part Three.) Your best bet is to get your GED and also have at least 15 hours of college credit. With most branches of the military, that will put you on the same footing as a high school graduate.

YES NO MAYBE I am interested in serving in the military because I have nothing better to do with my life.

- On the one hand, this is a terrible reason for joining the military. You need to think a lot more about what you are capable of and where you see yourself in the future. Joining the military should not be a spur of the moment decision or one made because you are bored or directionless. You must carefully consider all aspects of an enlistment decision and look for all options available to you, even if you aren't sure right now what those options are. Careful research will help you make the right choice for your future.
- On the other hand, the military is willing to take your raw material and mold you into the warrior it needs. If you are open to allowing yourself to be guided, the military can help you find a job and training while you figure out who you are and what you want out of life. Just be sure that you are willing to give them eight years of your life to do it.

YES NO MAYBE I am interested in serving in the military for the education benefits: money for college.

- Money is available for those who have served in the military and who now want to attend college. Make sure that you get information on how long you'll need to serve, what types of service are eligible, how much money you'll receive, and how and when that money can be used in the future. The next chapter offers information on the benefits of enlisting, including education benefits, and military recruiters will always be able to give you the most up-to-date information available. (More on talking to recruiters in Part Three.)

YES   NO   MAYBE   I am interested in serving in the military for the job benefits: training, housing, etc.
- The military is a great way to learn a career and get paid while you're learning. Remember, though, that the military's selection of jobs in the fields which interest you may be limited and/or the military may or may not find you qualified for training in the job you want. If you can't get the training that you're interested in, you can see if the military offers another job which you would be interested in doing or you will have to look for civilian training in the career you want.

YES   NO   MAYBE   I have computer, mechanical, scientific, medical, administrative, or technical interests or skills that I want to make into a career and need to be trained in.
- These are great skills to hone in the military, though if you aren't planning on making the military a life-long career, then you will want to look for a military job which will allow you to learn skills that you can use in civilian life after your term of service is up. Check out one of the books or websites on military jobs in the appendix under "For More Information — Career Planning." They will help give you an idea of what military jobs are available and how they correspond to civilian work.

YES   NO   MAYBE   I have artistic interests or skills that I want to make into a career and need training in.
- Many people assume that the military only offers technical jobs, but if you want a more artistic career, the military has jobs for you as well. There are some spots for chefs, musicians, graphic designers, and more in the military, but the number of these jobs available can be lower than other positions, so competition is often higher.

- If you are willing to delay your artistic career in favor of serving in the military, you can choose a different career path during your service and then use your educational benefits to study your art once you have left or retired from the military.

YES   NO   MAYBE   I want a job that can become a lifetime career.
- The military is a good possibility for a lifetime career. As long as you are willing to apply yourself to your work, you can retire after 20 or 30 years and still be young enough to enjoy yourself and even start a second career while also collecting your military retirement pay.

YES   NO   MAYBE   I need a job for now, but I am not sure that I want to make a life-long commitment.
- The military is also a great choice for those who want a job for now, but who aren't sure that they want to stay in that career forever. You'll have the opportunity to reenlist every few years and can decide at that time if you want to stay in or get out. If you decide to stay in, though, you're bound for the next few years, so the military is not a good choice for those who like to switch jobs every year. Consider what job you want to do and think about if you'll want to do it in the military for at least two, four, or six years, depending on how long your term of enlistment is.

YES   NO   MAYBE   I want a 9-to-5 job with a set schedule.
- Then the military is probably not for you. Military jobs can be orderly and set, with regular hours, but many of them involve working varied hours and an ever-shifting schedule.

YES   NO   MAYBE   I am a hard worker.
- If you are willing to work hard, then military life may be a good fit for you. Your superiors will want to see you giving your all and the service personnel you work with want to be working with someone who can be there for them to help carry the load.

YES   NO   MAYBE   I want to push myself and see what I can accomplish.
- A stint of service in the military is a good personal challenge. During your initial recruit training, what your instructors will want is for you to give your best effort, especially when you think you can't. Later on in military service, your superiors and your fellow service personnel will want you to be eager to try new things, to learn, and to grow in your chosen field.

YES   NO   MAYBE   I like physical exercise and activity.
- The military requires that its service members be physically fit in order for them to perform their jobs to the best of their ability. Each branch of the service has its own requirements for physical fitness standards, so you will need to consider whether or not you are able to meet or able to train to meet those standards.

YES   NO   MAYBE   I like being outdoors and/or don't mind roughing it.
- While not all military jobs are outdoors, at least during recruit training you will be hiking, camping, learning to navigate outdoor terrain, participating in warfare simulations, etc. If you are sent to war — which is a possibility for everyone who enlists in the military — then you will be faced with living in a variety of terrains, in tents and in other rough conditions. Even those personnel who live on ships or in barracks often live in close quarters with others and don't have many of the luxuries civilians may be used to.

YES   NO   MAYBE   I always do things my way and don't like taking orders from anyone.
- A big part of military life is taking orders, even if those orders seem to make no sense or go against what you may want to do. While the military does train its service members to think ethically and morally and to make judgments for themselves, it also expects people to follow orders and to work with others.

YES   NO   MAYBE   I want to be a leader or a manager.

- Military service is an excellent way to gain leadership experience. The military trains all its service personnel to take on leadership roles, even as early as boot camp. You have to be willing to start at the bottom, though. Don't assume that you will lead right away. You have to learn how and you have to earn the right to lead.

YES   NO   MAYBE   I work and play well with others.

- Teamwork is a major part of military life. Not only will you be working closely with others in your unit, you will also be living in close quarters — sometimes very close. The military needs people who can handle being around others and working in groups.

YES   NO   MAYBE   I like meeting new people and I can be open to diverse beliefs and opinions.

- Much of military life is meeting new people, whether it is other servicemen and women or people in other countries and from other cultures. Flexibility and openness are important qualities in a service member. The military does not tolerate discrimination and service men and women are expected to be able to be tolerant of the people — both military and civilian — with whom they have to work.

YES   NO   MAYBE   I like to travel.

- You will travel if you join the military, but remember that you won't always get to choose where you will travel to. The military will try to station you in locations where you want to go, but the military's needs always come first.
- If you join the Reserves or the National Guard (meaning you will be serving part-time, rather than on active duty which is full-time), then you will be assigned to a reserve unit in your area. This does not mean, however, that you won't travel. Reservists and National Guard members still travel for training or when they are called to war or to assist in relief operations.

YES   NO   MAYBE   I am a conscientious objector. I refuse to fight or participate in any war because of my religious, personal, moral, or ethical beliefs.

- Then you SHOULD NOT join the military. If you try to enlist, the recruiter will ask you if you are a conscientious objector. If you say yes, then you will ineligible for enlistment. If you lie, then you could face severe penalties later on if you object to being sent to war. The military is a fighting institution. It trains its members to fight, to wage war, and to kill. If any of these seem like they are something you cannot do with a clear conscience, then you should seek out other service options.

YES   NO   MAYBE   I am okay with some wars, but only if I agree with the government's reasons for waging them.

- The military exists to carry out government policy. Service personnel are expected to obey their superiors all the way up to the President of the United States, who is the Commander in Chief of the armed forces. Whether or not service members agree with those orders is immaterial. They still have to obey. While in the military you will retain your rights as a United States citizen and can use your vote to try to change government policy, but you will still be expected to fight in the wars waged by the United States until such time as that policy changes.

YES   NO   I have dependents.

- Dependents are any people that you have to take care of: your current spouse; any of your children or stepchildren who live with you or who you support, who are under 18 and unmarried; and any other family members who need you for more than half of their support. The branches of military limit the number of dependents that you can have because they require you to be able to adequately support them financially. Each branch has its own regulations about how many dependents you can have and whether or not having dependents will require you to get a waiver in order to enlist. Your recruiter can tell you more about the policies of his or her branch.

YES   NO   I am married.

- You can serve in the military while married, but you and your spouse should both know that military service can put a strain on your marriage. You may be away for long periods of time and face stresses that your spouse may not understand. You'll both have to work hard to make your marriage a success.
- If your spouse is already in the military, then you'll need to work with your recruiter and your superior officers to help you arrange to be assigned to duty stations near each other. You should also know that the military has strict policies on fraternization between officers and enlisted personnel, so if one of you is an officer and one is enlisted, this could cause problems during your time of service.

YES   NO   I am a single parent.

- The military will NOT allow you to enlist if you are a single parent with sole custody of one or more children. In order to enlist, you will have to give up custody of your child or children and then often wait several months to a year before being eligible to enlist. If you have joint custody of your child or children, then you will have to fully turn over custody to the other parent during the time in which you are in basic training. Additionally the other custodial parent will have to sign a statement agreeing to that arrangement before you are eligible to enlist.
- Those service members who become single parents while in the military find that single-parenting can often be incompatible with military service. The military requires that service personnel place their jobs before their families. They must be ready to deploy at a moment's notice and must have a local person who will sign a written agreement to take charge of their children with no prior notice. Any violation of a "Family Care Plan" will result in an immediate discharge.

YES   NO   MAYBE   I am not married and I don't have kids, but I want to have a family someday.
- You can have a family and serve in the military. Many military service men and women are married and have children. Most military bases have childcare facilities, schools, playgrounds, and family housing. There are no longer any regulations preventing women from being pregnant while on active or reserve duty and there are even special pregnancy uniforms. And the tight-knit military community means a built-in support system for your family.
- However, raising a family while serving in the military has its own special challenges. You will likely be away from your family for extended periods of time, missing birthdays, anniversaries, and holidays. Your family will have to move often, usually every three to five years, which means your children will have to change schools and your spouse will need a career where he or she can change jobs often. Military pay, especially enlisted pay and especially for lower ranking enlisted personnel, is not high and it can be tough to make ends meet. And military work puts you at risk for stress, injury, illness, and death, so you will have to make sure that your family is prepared for any eventuality.

YES   NO   I am female.
- Today's military could not operate without its female soldiers, sailors, Airmen, Coast Guardsmen, and Marines. Women serve in all five branches as both officers and enlisted. With the exception of some adjustments for physical qualifications, women are held to the same standards as men when enlisting in the services. That said, though, there are some things that women who are interested in serving should consider.
- First of all, women in the Air Force, Army, Marine Corps, and Navy are not eligible for all jobs. Combat jobs are off-limits to female service members and women are not allowed to serve in

18

the Special Forces, such as the SEALs. (The Coast Guard, however, has no gender qualifications on any of its career fields.) The military's restrictions do not mean that women do not see combat, though. Military women are still sent to war zones such as Iraq and Afghanistan and their duties there, as well as the fluid nature of modern warfare, often mean that they see as much combat as their male comrades.

- Second, all potential enlistees need to consider any children they currently have and whether or not they are likely to have children in the future. Women — and men — are allowed to serve in the military while also being parents, but there are many challenges that come with those dual roles. Read the information above about dependents, single parents, and family life in the military.

- Finally, enlistees should know that rape and sexual assault, of both male and female personnel, is a problem in the military. In April 2011, fifteen female veterans and two male veterans brought a lawsuit against the Department of Defense, charging that military commanders did not do enough to prevent sexual assault, to support victims, and to prosecute offenders. According to the Service Women's Action Network, over 3000 military sexual assaults were reported in 2010, though the Pentagon estimates that 70–80 percent of military sexual assaults are unreported. The military has policies about sexual harassment and offenders who are found guilty of rape and assault are dealt with, but many victims say that they are reluctant to bring charges against their attacker or attackers for fear that they will not be believed or that it will adversely affect their careers. The Pentagon is looking into the situation, but at this time it remains a serious issue.

YES   NO   MAYBE   I am homosexual or bisexual.
- In December 2010, President Barack Obama signed a bill into law which overturned "Don't Ask, Don't Tell," the policy which

allowed homosexuals to serve in the military only if they did not tell anyone their sexual orientation or participate in homosexual activities (i.e., sex or gay marriage). Though there was much back and forth in court about overturning the policy, it was finally repealed officially on September 20, 2011. As of that date, men and women serving in the military can no longer be discharged for admitting that they are homosexual or bisexual and potential enlistees are no longer considered ineligible if they are gay. (Transgender persons were excluded from the repeal and transgender persons are not eligible to enlist if they have had a sex change operation.) Service personnel who were discharged under "Don't Ask, Don't Tell" will be allowed to reenlist if they desire.

- Even before the repeal of "Don't Ask, Don't Tell," homosexuals were serving in the military. Estimates say that over 70,000 homosexual men and women are serving in the military as of May 2010 and over a million veterans are gay, lesbian, or bisexual. The repeal is expected to bring in roughly 37,000 new homosexual and bisexual enlistees.

- But even with the repeal of "Don't Ask, Don't Tell," there will still be years of work to do in order to insure that gay service personnel are openly integrated into military life. The first men and women serving openly will likely face harassment, tension, stress, and more, just as the first minorities and the first women did when they integrated into the military, though the military branches are working to insure that troops are trained in the policy that sexual orientation has nothing to do with the military's mission. If you are homosexual or bisexual, you are allowed to enlist and serve, but you will probably have to work even harder to prove yourself during your time of service. At this time the Pentagon is not planning on adding sexual orientation to its equal opportunity policy, so you will probably not have a legal way to fight discrimination and harassment which is based on your orientation.

- Additionally, the Department of Defense (DoD) is restricted by the 1996 Defense of Marriage Act, which limits marriage to that of one man and one woman, so partners of gay service members will not be eligible for certain spousal benefits, such as on base housing or medical coverage. And if even if you are legally married in a state that allows gay marriage, the federal government does not acknowledge your marriage for purposes such as filing taxes or receiving death benefits, so the military cannot recognize your marriage either. However, the Pentagon has ruled that military chaplains are allowed, if they so choose, to perform wedding services for homosexual couples in states where gay marriage is legal. There are likely to be more changes as policies are enacted that address the issues of gay service members.

YES   NO   I am not a United States citizen.
- You can only join the military if you are a United States citizen or if you are a legal permanent resident who has a green card and is living in the United States. The military will not help you immigrate and cannot help your family immigrate after you join. If you have lived in a country that is considered hostile to the United States, then you will have to get a waiver in order to be able to enlist. Additionally, job opportunities for non-citizens are more limited as you will not be eligible for the security clearances needed for some jobs. Once non-citizens have enlisted, however, there are accelerated programs that will help them become citizens.

YES   NO   I am currently having financial or legal problems.
- The military is not a way for you to escape your financial or legal obligations. You will not be allowed to enlist until you have cleared up any financial or legal issues, such as bad credit or scheduled court appearances. Some financial or legal problems could also affect your choice of military jobs, since they could hinder your ability to get a security clearance.

YES   NO   I have a criminal background or have had scrapes with the law in the past.
- You will need to talk with a recruiter about whether or not your past crimes will keep you from being eligible for military service. Criminal waivers are available in some cases, but the requirements vary depending upon the crime. All past brushes with the law will come to light during either the enlistment process or during a security clearance check, so you must not lie or omit information when talking to your recruiter.

YES   NO   I have a physical disability or serious health issue.
- Depending upon what that disability or illness is you may be ineligible for military service. There is a very long list of disabilities and illnesses that will make you ineligible. Recruiters can give you the complete and up-to-date list, as well as tell you if you might qualify for a medical waiver which will allow you to serve despite your medical history.

YES   NO   I am a drug user or have used drugs in the past.
- The military takes drug use very seriously. All service personnel are regularly tested for drug use. If you are thinking about enlisting and are currently using drugs, now is the time to get help and stop. You will not be able to continue using drugs while you are in the service. Even if all you use is tobacco, you will not have access to it during recruit training, so stopping now will make training easier for you.
- If you have used drugs in the past, even if you only experimented a single time, you will need to be honest about your usage when you talk with a recruiter. He or she can let you know if your drug use makes you ineligible for service or if you will need to apply for a medical or criminal waiver in order to enlist. This also goes for legal drugs which were prescribed for you by your doctor (such as Ritalin or antidepressants).

These are some of the things you should consider about your personality, your goals, and your past and present life. It is important to carefully consider all factors before making the decision to join the military. Think about your goals and whether or not a military career is compatible with them. If you want to learn a trade, does the military have jobs you can learn and then apply to a civilian career? Are you eligible for those jobs? What are the limitations on money you'll receive for education? How long will you have to enlist for? Consider all of the negatives and all of the positives of military service and decide if the negatives outweigh the positives for you. Now is the time to think clearly, rationally, and logically. Do your research and consider all options carefully.

Things to Consider for Parents of Potential Enlistees

If your son or daughter is considering joining the military, you will probably feel a mix of emotions. You may be proud that he or she is contemplating enlistment, especially if by doing so he or she is continuing a family tradition of military service. But you may also be worried. You may wonder if he or she will be tricked by a crafty recruiter. You may be concerned that your son or daughter may not be able to handle the rigors of basic training. You might fear for his or her life in facing the very real possibility of going to war or fighting. You may want him or her to do something different in life: go to college, get a civilian job, serve in another way. All of these feelings are normal and natural.

The most important thing to remember is that ultimately this is your child's decision. He or she must make the choice that is right for him or her. The military does not want enlistees who were coerced into joining and they don't want enlistees who haven't fully examined their reasons for enlisting. You and your child need to sit down together and discuss all of the options available to him or her. Calmly state your concerns and thoughts, but be sure that your child has enough time to say his or her piece. You need to know what he or she is thinking in order to help him or her make a decision. Here are some possible discussion questions:

- Why are you interested in joining the military?
- What other options are available to you? Can you go to school,

A mom and dad show off pictures of their children who serve in four different branches of the military (Official U.S. Army photograph by Kari Hawkins, USAG Redstone).

get a job, accept an apprenticeship, do mission work or service work for another agency, etc.?

- What opportunities does the military offer that you cannot get in college, in a private sector job, or in another service organization?
- What pros and cons do you see with military service? What will you gain and what will you have to give up with military service?
  - o Go over Chapter 1: Things to Consider with your child to help answer these questions.
- Are you interested in being active duty or in joining the reserves?
  - o Either way, he or she will still be gone for basic training and

any follow on training. But after that training is over, reservists return home and serve with a unit close to where they live, assuming there is a reserve unit near them.

- Are you thinking of doing just one tour of duty in the military or are you leaning towards making it a lifelong career?
  - Even one tour of duty is about an eight-year commitment, accounting for both active duty time and time spent in the inactive reserves. More information can be found in Chapter 1.
- Which branch or branches of the military are you interested in? Why do they appeal to you? What do they offer that the other branches do not?
  - Ideally potential enlistees will research all branches of the military before ever speaking to a recruiter, so that they will have an idea which branch or branches might be best suited to their interests and abilities. This book is specifically about the Army, but Chapter 5 has basic information about each branch and the other books in the series address the other branches.
- What job or jobs would you like to do in the military? Why is the military the best place to learn and practice that job or those jobs? Are there civilian opportunities to train and work in that field or those fields?
- Do you know anything about life in the military? What housing is available? What services are offered both on base and off? What hours will you work?
  - Military life varies widely depending on if a service member is on base or off, on a ship or not, active duty or reservist, junior enlisted or senior, what job he or she is doing, etc. If you and your family have the time, take a tour of military bases from all branches. Approach the tour as you would a college tour — look over the facilities, talk to people who are living and working there, ask any questions you have. The public affairs personnel on base can help you schedule a tour.

- What benefits — health, medical, financial, educational — does the military offer? What are the limitations attached to these benefits?
- Are you ready to deploy for months at a time if you are assigned to do so? Do you feel capable of dealing with the realities of war? Will you be able to fight and kill if told to do so?
- Have you spoken with any military personnel?
  - Help your child arrange to speak both with personnel serving right now and with retired personnel. Just remember that those who have retired will not have the most up-to-date information on benefits, jobs, life in the military, etc. But they will be able to tell your child how their service changed them for both good and ill.
- What are the enlistment requirements for each branch of the military? Do you meet those basic requirements?
  - Chapter 9 has the basic requirements for the Army.
- Do you feel academically ready to take the Armed Services Vocational Aptitude Battery (ASVAB) test? How can I help you prepare?
  - There is more information on the ASVAB in Chapter 13.
- Do you feel that you are in good enough physical shape for military training and service? Are you prepared to improve your physical fitness level so that you will be ready for basic training?
- Are you mentally ready to give up a lot of your personal freedom during your time in basic training and, to a lesser degree, while you are serving in the military?
- How will serving in the military affect your personal life? Is your boyfriend/girlfriend/husband/wife prepared for and supportive of you enlisting?
  - If your child is married, he or she should have his or her spouse look over Chapter 3: Things to Consider for Spouses.

- *If your child has children*: How will you support your children while you are in the military? Is your spouse prepared to be a part-time single parent? *If your child is a single parent*: What are the military's regulations on enlisting as a single parent? What family care plan will you put in place while you are training and serving?
  - Many branches of the military will not allow single parents to enlist. Most require them to give up custody of their children before they are allowed to join. While serving, parents must have a family care plan in place so that their children do not affect their ability to do their military job, which includes being able to be deployed at short notice.
- If you are unable to join the military for any reason, what would you do instead?
- Can I come with you when you meet with recruiters?
  - This will give you the opportunity to ask any questions or voice any concerns you might have. Remember, though, that your child's meetings with recruiters *must* be led by your child. He or she should do most of the talking and most of the responding to the recruiters' queries. You are only there in an advisory and supportive capacity. More information on meeting with recruiters can be found in Chapter 10.
  - NOTE: if your child is 17, then you will have to come with him or her to recruiter meetings and you will have to give your permission before he or she can enlist.

Your child may not have all the answers to these questions at first. The questions are designed to help him or her spot areas where he or she needs to do more research. The best thing you can do is to help him or her find out more about all aspects of military service. Look at both the pros and cons of enlisting. For some people the military is a rewarding lifelong career. For others it is a time when they are paid to learn a trade, while also earning money for their education and while giving back to their country. And some other people discover that military service is not for them. Maybe they have physical issues which preclude service or maybe they decide that their skills, interests, and goals do not mesh with military life. No matter what your child decides, even taking the time to consider military service will teach him or her a lot about who he or she is inside and what his or her goals are for the future.

Things to Consider for Spouses of Potential Enlistees

There are a lot of reasons why your husband or wife might be considering joining the military. Perhaps he or she has finally decided to follow a childhood dream of enlisting. Maybe he or she feels a call to service that can no longer be denied. If the job market in your area is bad or if your spouse does not have the appropriate training, education, or skills for the available jobs, then the military might seem like a good option which will allow him or her to support your family. But whatever your spouse's reasons for enlisting, you both need to sit down and talk carefully about what joining the military will mean for your family. Look over the questions for potential enlistees in Chapter 1. The questions will give you an idea of some of the things you and your spouse need to think about when he or she considers enlistment. Here are some other possible discussion questions:

- What opportunities does the military offer our family that we cannot get by you going to college, getting a private sector job, or joining another service organization?
- What pros and cons do you see with military service? What will we as a family gain and what will we have to give up if you enlist in the military?
- Are you interested in being active duty or in joining the reserves?
  - Either way, he or she will still be gone for basic training and any follow on training. But after that training is over,

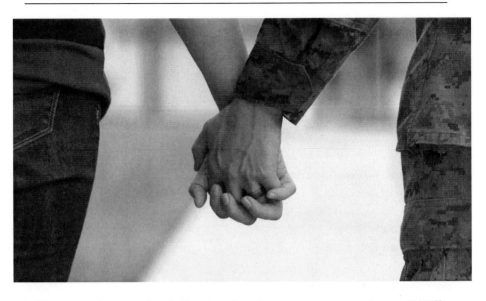

Military marriages can be challenging, but there are many rewards as well (Official U.S. photograph by Lance Cpl. Daniel Boothe).

reservists will return home and serve with a unit close to where they live, assuming there is a reserve unit near them.

- Are you thinking of doing just one tour of duty in the military or are you leaning towards making it a lifelong career?
  - Know that even one tour of duty is about an eight year commitment, accounting for both active duty time and time spent in the inactive reserves. More information can be found in Chapter 1.
- Which branch or branches of the military are you interested in? Why do they appeal to you? What do they offer that the other branches do not?
  - Ideally potential enlistees will research all branches of the military before ever speaking to a recruiter, so that they will have an idea which branch or branches might be best suited to their interests and abilities. This book is specifically about the Army, but Chapter 5 has basic information about each branch and the other books in the series address the other branches.

- What job or jobs would you like to do in the military? Why is the military the best place to learn and practice that job or those jobs? Are there civilian opportunities to be trained and work in that field or those fields?
- What are the enlistment requirements for each branch of the military? Do you meet those basic requirements?
  - Chapter 9 has the basic requirements for the Army.
- Do you feel academically ready to take the Armed Services Vocational Aptitude Battery (ASVAB) test? How can I help you prepare?
  - There is more information on the ASVAB in Chapter 13.
- Do you feel that you are in good enough physical shape for military training and service? Are you prepared to improve your physical fitness level so that you will be ready for basic training?
- *If you and your spouse have a child or children:* How will we support our child or children while you are in the military? What will it mean for me to be a part-time single parent while you are training or deployed? What family care plan will we need to put in place while you are training and serving?
- How will our family be taken care of in the event that you are injured or killed while training or deployed?
- What support services exist on base to help military spouses? Will I be left alone for long periods of time while you are gone? How will we keep our marriage strong while you are away?
- What is life in the military like? What housing is available? What services are offered both on base and off? What hours will you work?
  - Military life varies widely depending on if a service member is on base or off, on a ship or not, active duty or reservist, junior enlisted or senior, what job he or she is doing, etc. If you and your family have the time, take a tour of military bases from all branches — look over the facilities, talk to peo-

ple who are living and working there, ask any questions you have. The public affairs personnel on base can help you schedule a tour.

- What benefits — health, medical, financial, educational — does the military offer? What are the limitations attached to these benefits? Do they just cover the service member or do they cover his or her family as well?
  - See Chapter 4: Military Benefits for more information.
  - If you and your spouse/partner are a same-sex couple, you should know that at this time, the military does not offer many benefits to same-sex spouses/partners of military personnel.

These questions are a starting point for you and your spouse to be talking over the possibility of military service. They should help you both learn what areas you need to research further. As your spouse continues to look into the possibility of military service, help him or her. Go to the recruiters' offices with your spouse. (More information on visiting recruiters can be found in Chapter 10.) Help him or her study for the ASVAB and get in shape physically. Whether or not your spouse decides that military service is right for him or her, the journey into the enlistment process offers you the opportunity to learn more about each other and your goals and desires for the future.

Military Benefits

While military men and women give up a lot during their time in the service, they also receive benefits to help them out. Those benefits range from basic pay you receive for doing your job, to allowances for living expenses, to extras like educational benefits. The list of benefits is extensive and varies slightly by branch of service, years of service, job, and rank. You will never get rich working for the military, but the benefits you receive can, when used wisely, help you save money, get an education, and prepare for retirement and/or a civilian career. Your recruiter will have the most up-to-date information on benefits and during your time of service your commanding officers will keep you apprised of what benefits are available to you. There are several resources about military benefits listed in the "For More Information" section as well.

The major categories of military benefits afforded to service men and women are: pay, allowances, and incentives; vacation or leave time; housing and meal benefits; medical coverage; educational benefits; and more.

Pay, Allowances, and Incentives

Basic military pay is the same for all branches of the service, but varies by rank and years of service. An E-1 (the junior-most enlisted rank; a Private in the Army) with less than four months of active duty will make $1357.60 per month as of 2011, but as soon as he or she has over four months of active duty service, then pay will be $1467.60 per month. Enlisted service men and women who make it all the way to the top of the enlisted ranks (E-9, a Sergeant Major in the Army) make between $4600 and $5100 per month at this time. Military personnel are paid on the 1st and 15th of each month.

Military pay tables are available here: *http://www.dfas.mil/dfas/ militarymembers/payentitlements/militarypaytables.html.* Each year Congress decides whether or not to raise military pay. The latest military pay charts will be located at *http://www.dfas.mil* under the heading "Military Pay."

In addition to the basic pay, military service members receive allowances. Allowances help cover the cost of housing, uniforms, etc. Housing allowance is for military service members who decide to and are able to live off base. It is designed to help cover the cost of renting or buying a home. If you are stationed in an expensive part of the country or world, then you may qualify for a cost-of-living allowance in addition to the housing allowance. There is also a basic allowance for subsistence which helps cover the cost of food purchased off base. Your clothing allowance helps defray the cost of buying and maintaining your uniforms. After you are issued your initial uniform during basic training, you are given an allowance to help you replace parts of the uniform that have worn out or need updating. This allowance varies depending upon how long you have served in the military. There is also an allowance to help you cover the cost of military moves and an allowance you receive when you are assigned away from your family for a long period of time, usually longer than 30 days. Generally most allowances are not taxable, which means you do not owe the government money for them each year as you do with your pay.

Incentives are the broad range of special pay which some military personnel earn. Incentives may be given based on job, such as working on a submarine or working as a parachute jumper. There is incentive pay for military personnel on flying status and for those assigned on a ship at sea. You can earn incentive pay if you are a diver, if you are proficient in and work with a foreign language, if you are assigned to a foreign country, or if you are stationed away from your dependents for over 30 days and they cannot accompany you. Incentive pay is given for hazardous duty and for service in a combat zone. Additionally, if a military service member serves in a combat zone, then his or her pay received during that time may be exempt from Federal taxes.

Vacation or Leave Time

Military personnel do get time off and they earn vacation time — called "leave" — at a rate of 2½ days per month for a total of 30 days a year, but unlike in civilian jobs, when you are on vacation weekends are counted as part of your leave. However, you do not get to take your vacation whenever you would like. Your time off has to be approved by your supervisor and he or she can deny your request if the military decides they need you to keep working.

Housing Benefits

Most military bases have some form of housing available, but who can live there and whether or not there is room for everyone varies depending upon the size of the base, the location of the base, and other factors. Generally speaking, lower-rank (junior) enlisted personnel who are single must live on base in the barracks. These range from shared rooms with shared baths (much like a dorm room at a college) to small, apartment-like singles where you and another service member share living quarters, but have separate bedrooms and bathrooms. Living in the barracks not only means sharing, it also means you are subject to inspections (both announced and unannounced). If you are assigned to a ship for any reason, your living quarters will be much more basic. Ship's berths are generally communal, as are the bathrooms, and they are small, so be prepared to share.

Junior enlisted personnel are sometimes allowed live off base, but they will not receive a housing or food allowance, so it can be hard to afford it on their pay. As you rise up the enlisted ranks (generally around

Soldiers play basketball outside their barracks (Official U.S. Army photograph by Virginia Reza).

E-5 in the Army), you become eligible to live off base using a housing allowance to help you afford a place of your own.

Married service members can live on base in apartments, duplexes, or separate houses, depending upon what is available on base, what rank you are, and how big your family is. Families can also use their housing allowance to live off base. If you are married to another military member, things are a little trickier, especially if you are in different branches of the service. The military tries to station you together as best it can, but that "best" is usually considered to be at duty stations within 100 miles of each other. And even with the overturn of the "Don't Ask, Don't Tell" policy, gay service members and their partners/spouses are not eligible for married, on base housing.

Meal Benefits

When you live on base in the barracks or if you are assigned to a ship, then you will generally eat in the dining hall. You will receive a basic allowance for food, but most of that will go directly to the dining hall to pay for the meals you are supposed to receive. Personnel living off base or those in houses on base provide their own meals, though they also receive the subsistence allowance to help pay for food.

Medical Coverage

The military, like most employers, offers healthcare benefits to their personnel. Active duty personnel are completely covered for both medical and dental. Servicemen and women can also make sure their immediate family is covered as well, through the military's healthcare plan called Tricare. (Gay service members' partners/spouses are not eligible for coverage. Their biological or adopted children may be eligible, but stepchildren will not be.) Tricare has several different types of coverage. In some of those plans, immediate family members of active duty personnel are completely covered without any extra costs, but with some limitations, while other plans have a yearly deductible. Reserve military personnel are covered during the time they are on active duty, and they can purchase coverage for their family during those times, but otherwise they are not covered. Military retirees no longer get free medical care for life, as they were promised in the past, but they can still belong to Tricare. Your recruiter will have the most up-to-date information on healthcare costs or more information on Tricare can be found at *http://www.tricare.mil.*

Educational Benefits

Many people join the military because of the education benefits. In addition to the job training all military personnel receive, they also have access to programs which can help them earn a college degree, either while serving or afterwards. Through distance education programs, many military personnel can work towards a degree during their off-duty hours, though you should be aware that earning a degree this way takes longer than going to school full-time and in the military it can sometimes be hard to find off-duty time for classwork, depending on what your job is. Bases and ships often offer classes to their personnel, providing the space for professors and students to work. All of the military branches also offer tuition assistance which will cover the cost of classes and fees, though there are limitations on how much they will reimburse you per semester hour (generally around $250) and a cap on yearly reimbursements (generally $4,500).

The most well-known education benefit is probably the GI Bill. There are several variants of the GI Bill, but all new military enlistees are automatically enrolled in what is called the Post–9/11 GI Bill. This new version of the bill adds to and adapts the benefits offered, but still with the goal of helping military service members pay for college. You will usually use your benefits after you leave or retire from the military, though you can also use your benefits while on active duty or in the reserves. The Department of Veterans Affairs, better known as the Veterans Administration (VA), pays your GI Bill benefits directly to your college or university and also offers a stipend of up to $1000 per year to help you cover the cost of books. Veterans and reservists also qualify for a monthly housing stipend as long as they are attending school full-time and not using a distance education program. One new benefit with the Post–9/11 GI Bill is the ability for personnel who have served in the military for at least ten years to transfer their GI Bill benefits to their spouses or children. GI Bill benefits are limited to 36 months and must be used within 15 years of leaving active duty service. You must have been discharged from the service honorably in order to receive GI Bill benefits.

You do not have to be planning to go to a two- or four-year college to use your GI Bill benefits. The benefits also cover you if you are planning on taking a correspondence course, receiving flight training, participating in a non-college degree program (such as beauty school or truck driver training), accepting an apprenticeship, or doing on-the-job training (as in police academy training or plumbing). Your benefits can help you pay for training and can offer you supplemental income as you work your way to a new career.

The VA also has a program to support the children and spouses of military personnel who were killed in action or permanently disabled. It is called Survivors and Dependents Assistance. You can receive this benefit even if you are military yourself and it can be combined with the GI Bill benefits to give you up to 45 months of educational support. It cannot, however, be used for correspondence course training.

Additionally every branch except the Air Force has a type of college fund. These funds, sometimes referred to as a "GI Bill Kicker," are in addition to the amount that you will receive through the GI Bill. The amounts you hear mentioned in ads for the military (i.e. "$40,000 for college") are the amount you will receive through the GI Bill added to the amount you will receive from the college fund. You cannot receive the college fund without getting the GI Bill, but with the college funds it is the military branches, not the Veterans Administration, that decide who is eligible.

Other Benefits

There are a wide variety of other benefits open to military personnel. Bases often have "commissaries" (grocery stores) and "exchanges" (department stores) for personnel and their families to shop. These facilities are on base, do not charge sales tax, and usually have slightly lower prices than comparable stores in town, which can save you and your family some money and time when you are picking up essentials, though the selection can be limited depending upon the size of your base. Morale, Welfare, and Recreation services are available for personnel and their families and they include recreation centers (which offer everything from discount tickets to shows and attractions to classes to family fun programs), gymnasiums for keeping fit, child development centers for families where both parents work full-time, libraries, and more. And if you serve active duty for twenty years, then you can retire with most military benefits and military retirement pay.

5

The Branches of
the Military

If you decide that a military career might be a good fit for you, you'll then need to decide which branch of the service you might be interested in. You should to talk to recruiters from all branches of the service, even if you think you know which branch you want to join. They can give you an idea of what their branch has to offer, tell you about how their branch is structured and what the enlistment requirements and expectations are, and help you to find out if their branch is good fit for you in terms of its culture and its job offerings.

Which Branch to Join?

This volume focuses specifically on the Army, but before going into detail about the Army, we'll look at all of the branches of the military in general, each separately covered in the companion books. There are five branches of the military: the Army, the Navy, the Air Force, the Marine Corps, and the Coast Guard, from largest to smallest.

ARMY

The United States Army is the oldest of the United States' military branches, founded in June 1775, and also the largest. Its main job is to fight on land using ground troops, tanks, helicopters, artillery, etc. As of September 2010 there were 561,378 people serving on active duty in the Army (not counting cadets at the United States Military Academy): 94,128 officers and 467,248 enlisted. Of those numbers, 15,070 of the officers were female and 60,377 of the enlisted personnel were female, about 13 percent of the Army's force. The Army also has two reserve units: the Army Reserve, which is run by the federal government, and the Army National Guard. Each state maintains its own National Guard units, rather than them being controlled by the national government. In 2009, there were 645,394 personnel total in the Army Reserve and the Army National Guard.

Army Emblem (United States Army).

NAVY

The United States Navy was also founded in the summer of 1775, though it was disbanded after the Revolutionary War and not officially reinstated until 1794. The Navy is the United States' sea-based branch of the military. Its mission is to fight battles at sea using ships and submarines. The Navy works closely with the United States Marine Corps to

Navy Seal (United States Navy).

accomplish that mission. The Navy also uses its large aircraft carriers to launch air attacks and can launch land attacks using long-range missiles. In April 2011 323,745 personnel — 52,364 officers and 271,381 enlisted — were serving on active duty in the Navy (not counting midshipmen at the United States Naval Academy), with 8,184 female officers and 43,438 female enlisted personnel or almost 16 percent of the Navy. The Navy does have a Reserve component and 109,271 personnel were serving in the Navy Reserve in 2009.

AIR FORCE

The United States Air Force is the youngest branch of the military, formed after World War II by the National Security Act of 1947. It is the aviation branch of the military and uses its resources to defend the United States in the air and in space. It has a wide variety of aircraft for fighting, transport, bombing, rescue, etc. The Air Force is also responsible for all military satellites. In September ber 2010, 329,638 service men and women were active duty in the Air Force (not counting cadets at the United States Air Force Academy), with 66,201 officers and 263,437 enlisted. Women made up 19 percent of those numbers, with 12,363 women serving as officers and 50,946 women serving as enlisted. The Air Force has a Reserve component and there are Air National Guard units in each state. In 2009 there were 220,364 personnel serving in both.

Air Force Seal (United States Air Force).

MARINE CORPS

The United States Marine Corps started during the Revolutionary War, but wasn't officially established as a separate branch until 1798. The Marine Corps is closely connected with the United States Navy. The Marine Corps' mission of amphibious warfare — launching land attacks from sea — is a good complement to the Navy's sea-based mission. The Marines also train forces in ground combat and use aircraft

Marine Corps Seal (United States Marine Corps).

and helicopters to attack. They use the Navy for medical support and some administrative support. The Marines are a small service, with about 201,623 people serving on active duty in September 2010. At that time there were 21,307 officers and 181,134 enlisted, about 7.5 percent of which were female (3,054 officers and 12,203 enlisted). There is a Marine Corps Reserve, comprised of 95,199 personnel in 2009.

COAST GUARD

The Coast Guard, which began as the Revenue Cutter Service in 1790, plays a unique role in the United States military. They handle boating safety, law enforcement, search and rescue, and other tasks related to maritime security. Unlike the other branches of the military, which operate under the Department of Defense, the Coast Guard is part of the Department of Homeland Security, though during times of war control of the Coast Guard can be transferred to the Navy, if so ordered by the President. In September 2010 the Coast Guard

had 42,358 personnel on active duty: 8,508 officers and 32,837 enlisted, not counting cadets at the United States Coast Guard Academy. 5,552, or 13 percent, of these active duty personnel were women. There is a Coast Guard Reserve (with 9,399 personnel in 2009) and a volunteer, unpaid Coast Guard Auxiliary.

Even if you are positive that you only want to serve in the Army, it is to your benefit for you to learn

Coast Guard Seal (United States Coast Guard).

about each of the branches of the military. The different branches do not operate completely independently and if you decide to enlist in the Army it is very likely that you will find yourself working with service members from other branches.

Next, in Part Two, we'll talk more specifically about the Army, looking at its history as well as what career opportunities are available for you in the Army.

Two

General Information About the Army

The History
of the Army

The Army is the oldest branch of the military, tracing its roots back to before the United States existed. When the thirteen original colonies were founded, all of them had a volunteer militia and all of them except Pennsylvania had a standing militia which every able-bodied man between the ages of 16 and 60 was required to join. Many of these militiamen were called up to fight with British troops during the French and Indian War (1754–1763).

Revolutionary War (1775–1783) through the Mid–1800s

In 1775, the Continental Congress voted to raise a Continental Army, mostly made up of infantry (riflemen), to fight against the British Army. This was a volunteer army which absorbed many of the state militias into one Army commanded by General George Washington. A Board of War and Ordnance was established in 1776 to administer the Army. General Washington had learned during the French and Indian War that the British way of fighting in long lines of soldiers standing shoulder-to-shoulder did not work in America's dense forests and wildernesses. His Continental Army used a new technique called "open-order" fighting as part of their effort to defeat the British forces.

The Revolutionary War Army was often inadequately clothed, fed, and paid. They also faced disease, homesickness, and lack of discipline, leading to many desertions, which forced the Army to accept British prisoners and white servants into its ranks. At first General Washington, who was a slave owner, did not want to accept free black men, but necessity convinced the Continental Army to admit them, and by the summer of 1776 black men were serving in almost every battalion. They served as soldiers, camp servants, and even spies. There was even an all-black regiment, the 1st Rhode Island. Some women disguised themselves as men in order to fight, whereas others — often the wives of soldiers — acted as battlefield helpers.

In the late 1700s, the Army's role was still being developed by the government of the new United States. The Board of War and Ordnance was abolished in 1781 when the position of Secretary of War was created, but when the Revolutionary War ended in 1783, the Continental Army was disbanded. As the new nation began to establish itself, the government saw the need for a standing army, rather than continuing to rely on local militia forces. On June 3, 1784, the Confederation Congress passed a resolution establishing a small regular army. After the government was reorganized under the newly ratified Constitution, it created a Department of War in 1789 and adopted the Army into it.

The new Army fought Native American tribes, defeating the northwestern tribes at Fallen Timbers in 1794 and setting the stage for future use as a domestic police force. It also focused on building fortifications along the United States' coast as part of the work of the Army Corps of Engineers, which was officially established in 1802. Also in 1802, the United States Military Academy was founded at West Point, New York, with the original goal of training future Army officers in military engineering. Exploration of the West was on the minds of many in the United States during the 1800s. President Thomas Jefferson sent Captain Meriwether Lewis and Lieutenant William Clark on an expedition to the Pacific Coast in 1804. In 1805, Lieutenant Zebulon Pike was sent to explore the Southwest and in Colorado he saw the peak that now bears his name.

The Army fluctuated in size during the early 1800s and suffered from mismanagement in the high command. Despite those problems, the United States was victorious during the 1812–1815 war against the

British Empire concerning maritime shipping and trade, now called the War of 1812. But in order to succeed, the Army had to rely heavily on volunteers — which in some cases meant convicts and privateers — rather than being able to fight using just regular troops. Some of those volunteers were free black men, some who were already serving in Northern militias and some in areas in the South — specifically Louisiana — who were promised a bounty to sign up and serve in segregated units. They served with distinction, but were subjected to racism and forgotten once the fighting ended. After the war, Congress quickly disbanded all volunteer troops, except those needed to fight in the continuing skirmishes with Native Americans.

The 1820s was a time of development for Army officers, who began to focus on professionalism, education, tactics, service ethics, and other tasks. But low pay and even lower chances of promotion, combined with hard duty, meant that many young officers did not plan to make the army a lifetime career. The enlisted ranks were even less lucky. Made up mostly of laborers who signed up for economic reasons, enlisted troops suffered low morale, especially because of the harsh living conditions at the frontier posts which began to spread across the West. Additionally, though African Americans had served in the later years of the War of 1812, by order of the War Department in 1820, all blacks were banned from military service, a ban which continued until the Civil War.

The Army also began to act more and more as a type of police force, especially when administering the government's Indian policies. Army forces fought in the Black Hawk War (1832) against Sauk and Fox Indians and in the Seminole Wars (1818, 1835–42, and 1855–58) against the forces of the Seminole Indians in Florida. The lowest point of the Army's history came with their participation in the forced removal of the Cherokee, Creek, Choctaw, and Seminole peoples from the South to Oklahoma during the Trail of Tears (1838–1839). The Army also administered the Louisiana Purchase and conducted diplomatic relations.

The Mexican War (1846–1848), fought mainly over control of some of the lands in the American Southwest, was one of "firsts" for the Army: it was the first in which a volunteer army, rather than a militia

General — later President — Taylor receiving orders at the Battle of Resaca de la Palma during the Mexican War (Library of Congress, lithograph by Nathaniel Currier).

force, played a major part; it was the first fought far beyond the United States' borders; it was the first where steamships were used as troop transports; and it was the first in which the Army administered a military government over a conquered area. The Army Corps of Engineers also played an important role in the Mexican War by mapping and building roads, bridges, and fortifications, a role it would later reprise during the Civil War.

The Civil War (1861–1865), Reconstruction, and the Late 1800s

After the Mexican War, the United States was larger by over one million square miles, having added Texas, as well as the land that eventually became New Mexico, Arizona, California, Nevada, Utah, and parts of Colorado and Wyoming. But the nation was in turmoil over slavery and states' rights and the fighting with Native American tribes continued. John Brown, a fiery abolitionist, was run out of Kansas by Lieutenant James "Jeb" Stuart's Army forces in 1856 after he took revenge for a Missouri proslavery group's attack on Lawrence, Kansas. Brown later turned up in Virginia in 1859, raiding the armory at Harper's Ferry. He was caught there by Lieutenant Colonel Robert E. Lee and executed. By the time Abraham Lincoln was voted President of the United States in 1860, the nation was on the road to war.

When the Civil War began in 1861, the Army was torn apart. Over a quarter of the officers left to support the Confederacy. Though the Army called for volunteers, not enough men enlisted and by 1863 Congress established the first United States draft, requiring all men between the ages of 20 and 45 to register for military service. Though it began the war with only about 16,000 troops, by the end of the Civil War the Union Army had one million men. The Union was reluctant in the beginning to allow black men to enlist, even though they offered to serve right from the beginning of the war. But as the war dragged on, leaders realized the need for more soldiers and ultimately more than 186,000 African Americans served with the Union. Over 10,000 women were nurses, though some were doctors, still a new concept at the time. Dr. Mary Walker was even awarded the Medal of Honor for her service, still the only woman to have won it. Others acted as spies, protected their homes in guard units, or even disguised themselves as men in order to fight.

General Ulysses S. Grant led the United States Army to victory, later going on to become President of the United States, by defeating the Confederate forces led by General Robert E. Lee, who had once been offered command of the Union troops. The Civil War was a time of advancement in military tactics and technology. The Union Army used railroads, the telegraph, photography, reconnaissance balloons, and rifled artillery in their fight to win the war.

After the Civil War, the Army was tasked with military occupation of the former Confederate States. It was there to carry out federal policies aimed at Reconstruction, which ran from 1865 to 1877. The Army's tasks included peacekeeping, opening schools, repairing railroads and bridges, running banks, holding courts, maintaining election laws, protecting freed blacks, and controlling groups like the Ku Klux Klan. In the North and West during the late 1800s, the Army was used like a police force during labor strikes at factories. The Army also continued its tradition of completing engineering projects for the public good, building a system of levees to prevent flooding along the Mississippi River, lighthouses on the shores of the Great Lakes, and a system of telegraph wires. The year 1877 saw the graduation of former slave Henry O. Flipper from the United States Military Academy, the first black man to do so.

During this time the Army returned to its previous mission of patrolling in an effort to acquire much-desired Native American lands. Though Native Americans won some battles — probably the most famous is the Battle of the Little Big Horn (1876) — generals such as William Tecumseh Sherman and Philip H. Sheridan supervised as the Army slowly but surely forced the Plains Indians off of their land and into reservations. During this time, Congress authorized the creation of the first permanent units of black soldiers, led by white officers. (All-black units, as well as integrated black troops, had previously served in the Revolutionary War, the War of 1812, and the Civil War, but they were not permanent units.) As they participated in campaigns against the Native Americans in the 1870s, several of these units earned the name "Buffalo" Soldiers. One woman even served with the Buffalo Soldiers — Cathay Williams, who enlisted as a man named William Cathay and served for almost two years before her secret was discovered when she fell ill. The Spanish-American War (1898) ended the century on a low note. Though the United States won the territories of the Philippines, Puerto Rico, and Guam from Spain, the Army was not prepared for the conflict and more soldiers died of disease than were killed in battle.

The Turn of the Century, World War I (1914–1918), and World War II (1939–1945)

This failure motivated the Army to reorganize and refocus on training for world conflicts and modernization. The general staff system was adopted in 1903 and the Office of the Chief of Staff of the United States Army was set up. In 1901 women were allowed to join the Army Nurse Corps and in 1907 the Army established an aeronautical division as part of the Signal Corps in response to the Wright brothers' development of a successful engine-powered airplane. The Army Corps of Engineers began construction on the Panama Canal in 1904 and completed it in 1914, opening a new path from the Atlantic to the Pacific. The National Defense Act of 1916 had the goal of expanding regular forces, developing the Army reserve and expanding and strengthening the National Guard, as well as laying the groundwork for the Reserve Officer Training Corps (ROTC).

But even with these preparations, the Army was still under-prepared for World War I when the United States entered the conflict in 1917. The fighting in World War I was different than previous world conflicts. Trenches were dug in battle fields and troops would fight from within them, unable to cross into open ground due to barbed wire and artillery. New weapons were developed, including machine guns, tanks, airplanes, and chemical weapons, forcing military leaders to create new tactics to go with their new technology.

Congress passed the Selective Service Act of 1917 which made all able-bodied men between the ages of 20 and 30 eligible for military service. Ultimately more than four million men served in the Army in World War I. African American men signed up to be soldiers despite the Army's policy of racial segregation which forced many to serve in supply or labor jobs, rather than on the front lines. They served with honor despite the fact that they fought racism at home in addition to the battles on the frontline. The 369th Infantry Regiment, nicknamed the Harlem Hellfighters, was the first all-black U.S. combat unit to be sent overseas. They were assigned to the French army and during 191 days at the front, none of their men were captured and no ground was lost to the German army. This came at a cost of almost one-third of the men in the unit.

More than 20,000 women served as nurses and at least 220 women served as telephone operators under the Signal Corps (though these women were considered by the Army to be civilian contract workers). African American women were not accepted into the Army Nurse Corps until just after the war ended and they were later denied benefits because they did not serve during wartime.

At the end of World War I, Army troop strength was cut back drastically once again and by the mid–1930s the Army did not have a single combat ready division. But as the Nazis began to gain a foothold in Europe, leading up to World War II, Congress gradually began to increase the Army's size and to issue contracts which would encourage the weapons industry to develop the techniques to be able to rapidly increase arms production. After the Germans defeated France in 1940, Army reserves were called up and the nation's first peacetime draft — the Selective Training and Service Act of 1940 — required all men between the ages of 21 and 35 to register for a year of military service. (The age range was later expanded to 18 to 45 and the length of service changed to the duration of the war.)

World War II was fought on many battlefronts and the Army reorganized several times during the war in order to adapt. The Army fought all over Europe, as well as in North Africa and the Pacific. They utilized tanks, machine guns, hand grenades, and artillery pieces (large guns). The Army was a part of joint operations with other Allied military forces, including the landing at Normandy, France, in 1944 (D-Day), which was the greatest amphibious attack in history. The Army Air Forces was the aviation division of the military and its fighters and bombers were a large part of the Allied Forces' battle plan on both the European and Pacific fronts. The Army Corps of Engineers supervised the Manhattan Project, where Army scientists worked with civilian sci-

entists to develop the first atomic bombs and it was Army Air Forces' planes which dropped those bombs on Hiroshima and Nagasaki, Japan, ending the war in 1945.

Women were important parts of the fighting forces during World War II, thanks to Congresswoman Edith Nourse Rodgers' efforts. In May 1942, the Women's Army Auxiliary Corps (WAAC)—which later became the Women's Army Corps (WAC)—was established because of a bill she introduced. More than 99,000 women—including African American women who served in segregated units and Japanese-American, Puerto Rican, and Native American women—served as officers and enlisted personnel in the WACs, working in administration, and as nurses, electricians, air traffic controllers, and mechanics. The Women's Air Force Service Pilots (WASP) program was established to use white female pilots to transport planes between bases, freeing male pilots to fly fighting and bombing missions. Sixty-six Army and Navy women were prisoners of war for two-and-a-half to three years in the Philippines.

Many African American men served in the Army during World War II, at first just in segregated units commanded by white men, though by the end of the war the Army integrated some units out of sheer necessity. There were few black officers, though in 1940 Benjamin O. Davis, Sr., became the first African American general in the Army. African American men were also allowed to join the Tuskegee Airmen, a group of black pilots which flew over 15,000 sorties and almost 1,600 missions, including more than two hundred bomber escort missions over Europe between June 1944 and April 1945, during which time they did not lose a single bomber to the enemy. Japanese-American soldiers faced discrimination, segregation, restriction of duties, and other hardships, even if they had been serving before the war began. But despite those obstacles, Japanese-American men still signed up to serve their country—some volunteering from internment camps—and they served honorably in combat, intelligence, and other units.

Korean War (1950–1953) and Vietnam War (1957–1973)

The post–World War II era saw many changes in the structure of the United States military forces. The Army Air Forces split from the United States Army with the National Security Act of 1947, becoming the United States Air Force. The draft was discontinued in 1947 — only to be brought back in 1948 — and the Army began to demobilize and send home many of the eight million men who had served in World War II. Other changes began to shape the Army in new and different ways. The Women's Armed Services Integration Act of 1948 allowed women permanent status in the regular and reserve forces, though with restrictions on numbers and promotion levels which continued until 1967. The WACs continued until 1978, however, when male and female forces were combined. Executive Order 9981 was also drafted in 1948, ending racial segregation in the military, and by the 1950s African Americans were integrated into the regular Army.

In the early 1950s, United States forces joined South Korea in its fight against North Korea, who was being assisted by China. Even though the conflict ended without a clear victory, it gave the Army experience in training troops of many nationalities. As the 1950s and 60s progressed, the Army focused on developing its weapons and its tactical organization. The first atomic shell was fired in 1953, the Army launched the Explorer 1 Earth satellite into orbit in 1958, and in 1965 the first airmobile division was activated, with a goal of using helicopters and airplanes to support ground troops. The Army was also used to help control civil disturbances in the United States during the racial and social upheavals of the time. In the 1960s, the Army's reserve underwent a much needed reorganization, which gave it greater focus and a mobilization function of providing combat and service support, though these reforms did not go into place until after the Vietnam War.

The Vietnam War was a conflict between forces in South Vietnam and those in North Vietnam, which were supported by the Soviet Union and China, as well as the Viet Cong rebels in South Vietnam. Starting in the mid–1950s, the Army contributed advisors to the South Vietnamese government, but by 1965 Army units began to head to war, using the draft to increase troop numbers. One of the successes of the Vietnam War was the use of the airmobile division. Helicopters were used as a major weapon to attack the enemy, transport cargo, and as an ambulance to evacuate the wounded. At the beginning of the Vietnam conflict, the Army was at the peak of its training, administrative efficiency, troop morale, and popularity among the citizens of the United States, but the drawn-out, unpopular war ended all that. By the time the Army withdrew from Vietnam in 1973, the quality of leadership had deteriorated, morale was extremely low, and drug abuse, violence, racial tensions, assaults on leaders, and defiance of authority were all prevalent, and scandals like the 1968 massacre at My Lai had tarnished the Army's reputation.

1970s through 1990s

During the late 1970s through the 1990s, the Army and the other military branches found themselves in a period of change. The draft was ended in 1973 and the military became an all-volunteer service. The Army dedicated itself to reorganization, planning to cut personnel and costs and to improve training and preparedness for war. Working to overcome the Army's drug, discipline, and race problems, leaders began programs designed to interest well-educated young people in military service. Women were integrated into the service, leading to the dissolution of the WACs as a separate Corps of the Army in 1978, and into all specialties except those of ground combat and special forces. The first women graduated from the United States Military Academy in 1980. In 1989, Army General Colin Powell became the first African American chairman of the Joint Chiefs of Staff, the body which oversees all United States military branches.

A focus on new weaponry starting in the 1980s allowed the Army to develop as a highly mechanized, fast-moving force with more artillery, aviation, and air defense capabilities. These new skills were put to the test when the Army assisted in conflicts in Grenada (1983) and Panama (1989). The Army also fought in or assisted during wars in the 1990s. Iraq invaded its neighbor Kuwait in August 1990, leading to the first Persian Gulf War in January 1991. During the several weeks of war, the Army outfought an Iraqi army which had been thought to be formidable. When land forces invaded in February, the Iraqi troops began withdrawing from Kuwait in just two days. The first Persian Gulf War was the first where Army reservists and National Guardsmen went to war in identifiable units, which helped them receive media attention and public acclaim. During the same time, the Army also assisted as peacekeepers in Somalia, Haiti, and the Balkans.

Recent History

Following the terrorist attacks of September 11, 2001, Army National Guard and reserve personnel were called up to act as security personnel at military bases, in airports, and on sites that could be targets for terrorist attack, such as bridges, ports, and power plants. On October 7, 2001, the United States military began a campaign in Afghanistan against Al-Qaida and Taliban forces. The Army had fifty thousand soldiers in the area by November 8. They worked with local forces and other United States military personnel to overthrow the Taliban government.

In the second Persian Gulf War, which began in 2003, the Army participated in a United States–led invasion of Iraq. Ground troops moved in from neighboring countries, mostly Kuwait, and other Army forces parachuted into the northern part of Iraq to join Kurdish rebels. The Army helped bring about the fall of the capital of Baghdad, leading to the end of the rule of Iraqi dictator Saddam Hussein and his Baath party in 2003. Army engineering divisions worked to build secure roads and facilities to support the Army's operations. The first Medal of Honor

A Blackhawk helicopter flies past a damaged mosque in Iraq (Official U.S. Army photograph by Staff Sgt. Lynette Hoke).

of Operation Iraqi Freedom was awarded to Sergeant First Class Paul R. Smith, with Company B, Eleventh Engineer Battalion.

The Army pulled out of Iraq in December 2011 and is now focused on completing its mission in Afghanistan. It continues to develop its fighting techniques, weapons, machinery, and technology to meet the changing shape of warfare, aiming to face down future threats to the United States and overcome them.

Career Opportunities in the Army

Obviously one of the most important things you should consider when you begin comparing the different branches of the military is what jobs will be available to you in each branch. The recruiters you visit will help you learn about the career fields available in each branch, but you will be better off if you do some research before you enlist. That way you will know which job fields appeal to you and be able to make the decision that is right for your future.

What if you already know exactly what military career field you want to be in? You should still look at everything that is available. Many factors can prevent you from entering a particular field — the military may have too many people already doing that job, your test scores may show that the job is not a good fit for you, that job may not be open when you are ready to begin training, or the job may have restrictions which you cannot meet. If you have already looked at all the jobs available in each branch, then you can decide if you want to try for another job or if another branch may offer you a better chance to achieve your dream.

What if you don't know what military career field you might be interested in? Reading over all of the options available in each branch might give you some ideas, but your recruiter can help as well. The Armed Services Vocational Aptitude Battery (ASVAB) test that you take during enlistment will show you and your recruiter what career fields you are best suited for. (We'll talk more about the ASVAB testing process in Part Three.) Also, each branch of the military will have jobs that they are eager to fill. Your recruiter can tell you what those are and if you are qualified. So if you truly don't care what job you do, then you can allow yourself to be placed in one. But that should be a last resort only undertaken if you truly don't care whether you are a chef or a mechanic or a human resources specialist or something else completely.

The type of job you want to do might depend upon whether you want to work in a hands-on field or if you prefer a field where you are dealing with abstract concepts such as information, numbers, or words. You also want to think about if you prefer primarily working with machines or primarily working with people. Do you want to be in an exciting, ever-changing, possibly dangerous career or do you think you'd rather have a job with more stability? Are you more of a science and math oriented person or more of an arts and letters oriented person? These are all things to keep in mind as you consider the types of jobs the different military branches have to offer.

Your recruiter can tell you which jobs are open to you. At this time, women are not allowed to sign up for jobs designated as combat positions, though the United States government is considering changing that rule. (However, this doesn't mean that women in the military don't see combat. Many female service personnel serve in jobs that still send them into danger and near or even into the frontlines.) Some jobs are not open to enlistees who will be going into the reserves — only active duty personnel may fill those jobs — and reservists are usually limited in jobs depending upon the needs of their assigned unit. Other jobs, such as Special Forces, are not ones you can be guaranteed. If you meet the qualifications for consideration, you will be evaluated during your early training to see if you are a good candidate.

Whatever career field you pick, in whichever branch of the military, you will be working in that career field for at least the next four to eight years, so it is in your best interest to pick something that you think you will enjoy. If you enlist, the military is going to spend a lot of time and money training you, so it wants you to be in a job where you will work hard and excel. In Part Three you will learn about talking with your recruiter about your job possibilities. For now, let's look at what types of jobs are available in the Army.

Army Enlisted Careers

As the largest branch of the military, the Army has the greatest number of career choices. You can choose from jobs in a variety of fields:

- Combat Jobs
- Weapons Jobs
- Vehicle and Materiel Jobs
- Construction and Engineering Jobs
- Computers and Data-based Jobs
- Intelligence Jobs
- Jobs working with People
- Medical Jobs
- Safety and Security Jobs
- Public Affairs and Arts Jobs

Working in Combat jobs

When most people think of the Army, they think of the frontline soldier charging into battle. This type of job is still available, though combat soldiers today use the latest technology to win wars and complete their mission. Men who want the traditional soldier job might consider being an Infantryman. Training as an Infantryman is the starting point for those men who want to try to join such elite groups as the Special Forces, Airborne, Rangers, Snipers, and more. Cavalry Scouts are responsible for doing reconnaissance through uncertain territory. Other combat soldiers make up mortar squads or operate tanks or are responsible for front-line intelligence work. Though women are banned from many combat jobs by law, if you female and are interested in a combat position, talk with your recruiter about what jobs are open to you.

Working with Weapons

Weapons are an important military resource. Soldiers are needed for work on weapons such as howitzers, Multiple Launch Rocket Systems (MLRS), the AVENGER System, and the PATRIOT Missile Sys-

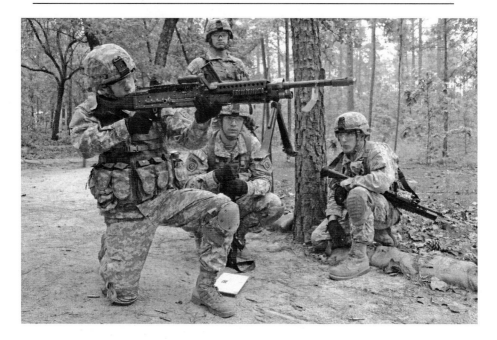

Infantrymen practice their shooting skills while on a field training exercise (Official U.S. Army photograph by Pfc. Jared Gehmann).

tem. Other soldiers specialize in ammunition, keeping track of the Army's stock of bullets, missiles, rockets, and more. Just as with any other mechanical device, weapons break down and need repair. There are soldiers who specialize in repairing weapons, from small arms and artillery to fighting vehicles like the Bradley to the PATRIOT and AVENGER Systems. If you would rather learn how to get rid of weapons, then you might be interested in the dangerous and challenging job of Explosive Ordnance Disposal. Soldiers who work in that field detect and render inoperable all types of unexploded bombs and devices.

WORKING WITH VEHICLES
AND MATERIEL

The Army has a large number of vehicles for use in completing its missions, as well as moving supplies and personnel. Soldiers are needed

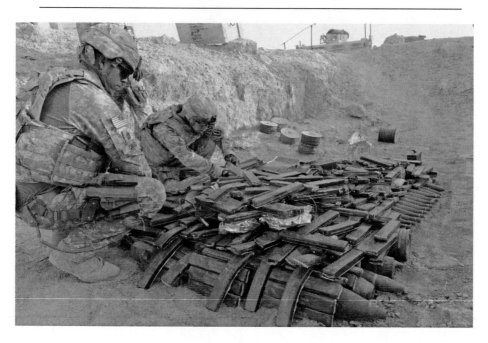

Explosive ordnance disposal specialists prepare to destroy weapons seized during the Iraq War (Official U.S. Army photograph by Staff Sgt. Nancy Lugo).

to repair everything from airplanes to watercraft. You can learn to fix helicopters, tanks, other track vehicles, and wheeled vehicles. Mechanics are needed to work on every part of the Army's aircraft. There are repairers who specialize in avionics (the aircraft's security, navigation, and flight control), aircraft structural parts (the body of the plane), aircraft electronics, and all other systems of both manned and unmanned aircraft.

Vehicles don't just need repairing, though. Motor Transport Operators are responsible for the operation of wheeled vehicles, as well as any cargo or passengers they might be assigned to carry. Other soldiers are Watercraft Operators, piloting, navigating, and maintaining the Army's fleet of landing ships. Acting as support for the Army's pilots are Air Traffic Controllers, who coordinate the landing and take-off of airplanes and helicopters. Parachute Riggers do the important work of

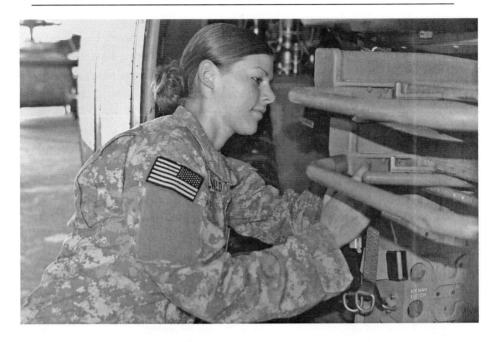

Keeping the Black Hawk helicopter running smoothly and safely is an important part of this mechanic's job (Official U.S. Army photograph by Spc. Alun Thomas).

making sure that parachutes are packed and prepared to the highest degree of accuracy to ensure the safety of all who fly Army aircraft. Soldiers also operate unmanned aerial vehicles used in reconnaissance and intelligence.

The Army needs a lot of supplies to keep running effectively and soldiers are responsible for organizing, ordering, taking care of, and shipping those supplies. Cargo Specialists make sure that cargo, people, vehicles, and other supplies get to where they need to be, whether by land or air or sea. Unit Supply Specialists are the soldiers who are in charge of the maintenance of all of the Army's supplies and equipment. Soldiers also work as Shower/Laundry and Clothing Repair Specialists, insuring that their fellow soldiers have clean linens, clothes, and shower facilities. This is especially important for soldiers fighting on the frontlines, where clean facilities can be hard to come by.

Working in Construction and Engineering

If you have ever longed to be part of a construction crew, then you can still pursue that dream in the Army. Soldiers work in all aspects of construction, from carpentry and masonry to metal work, plumbing, heating and air conditioning, and water treatment. There are soldiers who drive heavy construction machinery and soldiers who are responsible for quarrying (drilling, crushing, and grading gravel and rock). Other soldiers learn to install, maintain, and repair the many cables, RADAR, and other communications, data, and computer systems needed on bases. Soldiers are also needed to fix the Army's construction equipment and to be in charge of the Army's supply of petroleum fuels.

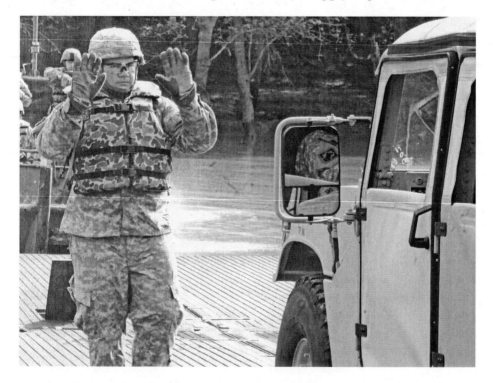

A Bridge Crewmember directs a Humvee onto a newly assembled temporary bridge (Official U.S. Army photograph by Sgt. Michael Behlin).

Army Divers complete building projects under the water and also patrol for dangers beneath Army vessels.

Working in an engineering job means that you are helping to build, repair, and improve all of the Army's facilities and resources. Men who want to combine fighting and construction might consider becoming a Combat Engineer. These soldiers construct fighting positions, obstacles, defensive positions, and place explosives for detonation. Other soldier engineers make maps, do land surveys, and draw up plans for Army construction projects. Soldiers working in labs do research to identify defects in metal equipment or to align, troubleshoot, and calibrate equipment. You might be interested in working as a Bridge Crewmember, building bridges and providing rafts so that your fellow soldiers can cross both wet and dry gaps in the land.

WORKING WITH COMPUTERS AND DATA

The Army's focus on technology means that many soldiers are needed to install, operate, analyze, and repair the Army's computer and data systems. You may be working to fix detection systems such as night vision equipment or nuclear, biological, and chemical warning and measuring devices. Soldiers work on radio receivers and transmitters, communication equipment, strategic and tactical systems, cable systems, and telephone systems. Some soldiers work on computer networks. They may develop software or install hardware. Still others are responsible for gathering weather data so that artillery units can target accurately.

WORKING WITH INTELLIGENCE

Closely related to jobs working with computers and data are jobs working in intelligence. Intelligence is the information gathering which allows the Army to protect the United States and complete its missions. Soldiers who are analysts are in charge of gathering intelligence data by studying photographs, electronic information, communications, and

A data specialist performs a systems check on her task force's information network (Official U.S. Army photograph by Sgt. Brandon Little).

other types of signals. Some soldiers are responsible for detecting and tracking ground targets, ships, missiles, and aircraft in order for the Army to prevent or prepare for attacks. Other soldiers focus on gathering intelligence from human beings through operations, debriefings, and interrogations. There are soldiers who specialize in translation and interpretation and there are soldiers who specialize in counterintelligence, working to detect and thwart threats to national security.

Working with People

While all of the jobs in the Army require that you be willing and able to work well with others, there are some jobs in which people, rather than equipment or vehicles, are your main focus. The Army needs people to act as human resources staff, assisting, advising, and keeping

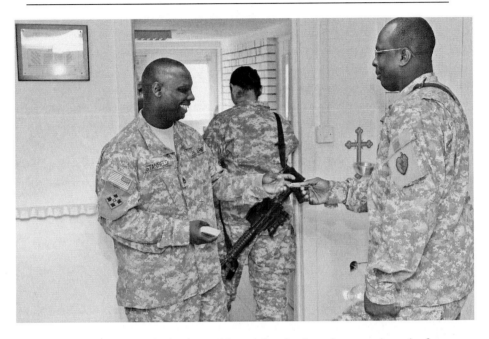

Chaplain's assistants help lead worship services both on bases and on the front lines (Official U.S. Army photograph by Staff Sgt. Tim Meyer).

track of soldiers and their dependents. Other soldiers are responsible for keeping the financial records of the Army. Soldiers who are Food Services Specialists make sure that their fellow soldiers are well-fed. If you are interested in serving both your country and your faith, you might be interested in being a Chaplain Assistant, helping the Army's Chaplains meet the religious needs of your fellow soldiers.

WORKING IN MEDICAL FIELDS

All of the Army's personnel and their dependents will need medical care at some point in time. Many soldiers work in medical careers, some directly working with patients and others working in a laboratory situation. Enlisted soldiers can work as dental hygienists, surgical assistants, pharmacy technicians, x-ray technicians, or assistants to physical therapists, nutritionists, eye doctors, mental health staff (psychiatrists,

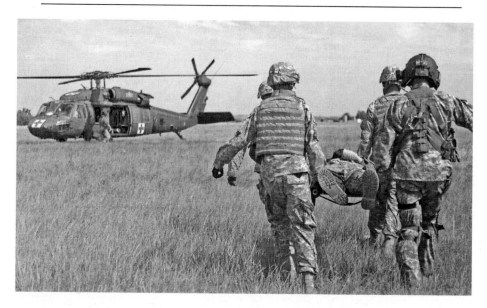

Medics transport a wounded soldier to a waiting Medevac helicopter (Official U.S. Army photograph by Spc. Levi Spellman).

psychologists, social workers, and mental health nurses), or even veterinarians. If you work in a laboratory, you might be an Optical Laboratory Specialist, making and repairing eyeglasses, or you might work in a medical laboratory, doing medical tests for patients. Soldiers who are Patient Administration Specialists keep medical records, while those who are Preventative Medicine Specialists are in charge of preventing the spread of disease. There are also opportunities for those who want to learn to repair and maintain biomedical equipment or for those who want to be Mortuary Affairs Specialists, helping with the final affairs of dead soldiers and their dependents.

Working in Safety and Security

Emergencies and security situations can occur at any time and the Army wants to be ready for them. Soldiers are trained to be firefighters and military police. Internment/Resettlement Specialists are in charge of military prisons and prisoners. Also working in law enforcement are

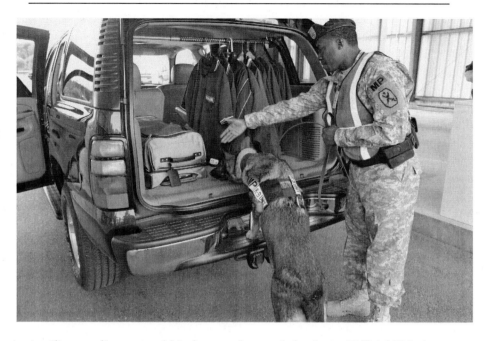

A military policeman and his dog search a truck for drugs (Official U.S. Army photograph by Mrs. Jennifer Bacchus).

soldiers who are Paralegal Specialists, assistants to military lawyers. Soldiers working as Civil Affairs Specialists are responsible for working with civilians in warzones and in areas where natural disasters and other emergencies have occurred. They make sure that civilians aren't injured in fighting, that they don't interfere with military operations, and that they get humanitarian aid as needed.

WORKING IN PUBLIC AFFAIRS AND THE ARTS

There are also careers in the Army for enlisted personnel who are creative and artistic or who like to organize and distribute information. Public Affairs Specialists present Army information through newspapers, magazines, the Internet, and through civilian news media. Psychological Operations Specialists have a similar job, but they work with foreign

Musicians are also a part of the Army (U.S. Army).

populations. They create and distribute information to influence populations as part of Army operations. Other soldiers work in radio and television broadcasting, helping to produce radio and film programs for the Army. Multimedia Illustrators are the graphic designers of the Army and there are many Army bands that need talented and experienced musicians.

Whatever your interests, there is an Army career that might be a good fit for you. The next step is to talk to a recruiter. Part Three will give you all the tips you need to know to begin the enlistment process.

THREE

The Enlistment
Process

What Is the Enlistment Process?

The enlistment process is the steps that take you from civilian to military recruit. It is an important process, filled with decisions that need to be considered soberly and at length. The choices you make during the enlistment process will shape your life for at least the next eight years and should shape the rest of your life, assuming you take full advantage of the training and educational opportunities afforded you during your military service. That means that you need to think carefully about all the options presented to you. You will receive a lot of information and advice from the recruiters you speak to, from your friends and family, and from research you do yourself. It is your job to compile all of that information and advice into a complete picture of what your options are. Until you give the Oath of Enlistment as you are leaving for basic training you are not obligated to anything, so take your time and make the decision that is right for you.

There aren't clearly defined steps that make up the enlistment process, since the experience is different for every recruit and the process varies depending upon which branch of the service you choose to enter. But there is a rough outline that each enlistment process will follow:

- Researching the different branches of the service and getting a general idea of what they are like
- Speaking with recruiters from all branches of the service
- Deciding which branch you are most interested in
- Completing paperwork detailing your past medical, legal, finan-

cial, and academic history to make sure that nothing in your past would prevent you from enlisting

- Taking the Armed Services Vocational Aptitude Battery test (the ASVAB) to see if you are qualified for that branch and to see which jobs you qualify for
- Visiting a Military Entrance Processing Station (MEPS) to get your physical
- Resolving any final physical, moral, or other waivers needed before being accepted into your chosen branch
- Taking the oath to enter the Delayed Entry Program
- Using your time in the Delayed Entry Program to get into physical and mental shape before basic training
- Visiting MEPS to take the Oath of Enlistment and leave for basic training

In this part, we are going to break down the enlistment process into easy to follow sections. First we'll talk about the basic eligibility requirements for entering the Army. Next we'll discuss who recruiters are and what you can expect when you visit them. Then we'll cover the basics of the Armed Services Vocational Aptitude Battery test (the ASVAB). We'll move on to talk about Military Entrance Processing Stations and what happens in them. Finally we'll talk about the Delayed Entry Program and how to use it to get yourself in the best possible shape, both mentally and physically, before you leave for basic training.

Eligibility Requirements

Gone are the days when a recruiter could sign up an unwary young man in the morning and have him ship off to basic training in the afternoon. Today's military requires that its enlistees meet a lengthy list of requirements. In order to see if you meet those requirements, your recruiter and the personnel at the Military Entrance Processing Station (MEPS) you visit will look at your mental, physical, and moral qualifications. You will have to fill out an application, submit medical documentation, undergo a physical, and more. This is done so that the military is certain it is selecting the brightest and best young men and women to serve. Even minor physical or moral issues can become major problems on a battlefield and the military wants to catch them before that happens.

Before you even meet with an Army recruiter, you can get an idea of whether or not you might be qualified to enlist. The basic eligibility requirements are what a recruiter looks at when he or she meets you for the first time.

Basic Requirements

- Be between the ages of 17 and 34
  - 17-year-olds need their parents' permission to enlist
- Be a United States citizen or a legal permanent resident
  - There are some restrictions on immigrants from countries deemed hostile to the United States
  - Non-citizens will not be eligible for jobs requiring security clearances

- Be a high school graduate
  - Only a very few GED holders are allowed into the Army each year
  - Your chances of enlisting with a GED increase if you have 15 or more college credit hours
- Score at least a 31 on the Armed Services Vocational Aptitude Battery (ASVAB) test
  - Or at least a 50 if you have a GED (more information on ASVAB scores in Chapter 13)
- Be 60–80 inches tall if you are male or 58–80 inches tall if you are female and able to meet the established weight standards for your height
  - The male weight standards can be found at *http://usmilitary. about.com/od/army/l/blmaleweight.htm*
  - The female weight standards can be found at *http://usmilitary. about.com/od/army/l/blweightfemale.htm*

If you do not meet these basic requirements, then you will more than likely not be able to continue with the Army enlistment process. Each branch's enlistment requirements are a little different, so if you do not qualify for one, you can always try to apply for one of the others. But the basic requirements are similar enough that you are better off trying to fix the issues that make you ineligible, such as your weight or your score on the Armed Services Vocational Aptitude Battery (ASVAB) test.

Alternatively, you can see if there is a waiver which would allow you to enlist despite not meeting some of the requirements. But waivers are a lot of work for recruiters and other military personnel, so they only want to do them for potential enlistees who are outstanding in other ways, such as those who speak a needed foreign language or who have extremely high ASVAB scores.

In addition to the basic eligibility requirements, there are some other factors to be considered. These can make you ineligible for Army service or might require a waiver in order to allow you to enlist (more on waivers in Chapter 12).

Other Eligibility Factors

- Tattoos: The Army does not allow you to enlist if you have tattoos that can be seen in an Army dress uniform or any above the bottom of the earlobe. Tattoos must not be racist (including rebel flags), discriminatory, or gang related (including praying hands). Command must approve any tattoos before you will be allowed to enlist. If your tattoo has foreign symbols or words the Army will verify the translation of those symbols or words to make sure your tattoo really says what you think it says.
- Body piercings: Females are allowed one hole in each earlobe. Otherwise body piercings must be removed and the holes healed (in the case of ear plugs and the like) before you are eligible for enlistment.
- Dependents: If you have two or more dependents (children) under the age of 18, then you will likely need to get a waiver to enlist in the Army. Single parents with sole custody of their children are ineligible to enlist. In order to become eligible, you must go through the courts to give up custody of your child or children and be without custody of them for one year before beginning the enlistment process. Single parents with joint custody must have the approval of the other parent in order to enlist. The other parent must agree to care for the children during basic training.
- Drug and alcohol use: You are ineligible to enlist if you use illegal drugs and/or abuse alcohol. Your recruiter will ask about all previous drug use and you will be given a drug test as part of your enlistment physical and at basic training. You should answer truthfully about all drug use, even casual experimentation. Your recruiter will be able to tell you if your prior drug use makes you ineligible or if a waiver will be required in order for you to enlist.
- Prescription drugs: You are likely ineligible to enlist if you are dependent upon prescription drugs, including insulin and

ADHD medications. Your recruiter will have more information on which drugs may disqualify you for service and how long you will need to be off of them before being eligible for enlistment. But *do not* discontinue any legal use of prescription drugs without the consent of your primary physician.

- Medical history: Certain medical conditions will prevent you from enlisting. You will be required to reveal your medical history to the military and you will undergo a physical during your enlistment process. The doctors examining you will determine if any medical conditions are temporary (meaning you can enlist once your condition improves) or are disqualifying (meaning you cannot enlist or that you will need a waiver in order to do so).

- Criminal history: Some criminal convictions will render you ineligible for military service. You must disclose any prior criminal history (even sealed juvenile records) to your recruiter in order to apply to enlist. He or she will be able to tell you whether or not your criminal record makes you ineligible or if you will require a waiver to enlist.

All of these eligibility factors are considered when the Army is making the decision on whether or not you are eligible for enlistment. Some factors cannot be waived and will prevent you from enlisting, but these factors can vary between the branches. So if you are still interested in military service, but cannot enter the Army, you should still speak with recruiters for the other branches and see if you might be eligible to serve with them.

Improving Your Chance for Eligibility

Before you begin the enlistment process there are some very simple steps you can take to make yourself a more eligible candidate.

- Finish school and further your education:
  - *If you are still in high school, stay there.* Do not drop out and do not waste your time. Study. Do your homework. Make

decent grades (aim for at least a C+ average in all of your classes and you will do fine when you take the ASVAB). Try to take a mix of basic classes (math, science, English, history) and more technical ones or ones related to a field you might be interested in (computers, business, journalism, etc.).

o *If you have finished high school, take classes at your local community college.* General education classes (math, science, English, history) will not only keep your mind fresh for the ASVAB, but getting them done now will save you time later if you decide to work towards your degree while serving in the military. Take your classes seriously, though, and strive to make decent grades.

o *If you have dropped out of high school, you MUST get your GED before you can even consider enlisting.* Additionally, it is recommended that you have 15 credit hours of college classes under your belt. This will put you on the same consideration level as a high school graduate.

• Visit your family physician:

o *You should get a full physical out of the way before beginning the enlistment process.* Not only will this alert you to any problems which might hold up your enlistment, but your family doctor can advise you whether or not you can stop taking any drugs that have been prescribed for you. He or she can also tell you how to get in shape for enlistment.

• Exercise and eat right:

o *According to a 2010 study at Cornell University, almost 12 percent of young men and over 30 percent of young women who are the right age for enlistment are ineligible due to not being able to meet weight standards.* Now is the time to lose weight, eat right, and exercise more. Your doctor is the best guide for this process. Never try to lose weight or begin an exercise program without consulting him or her first. Now is also a good time to stop smoking. It will improve your health and make you a stronger candidate.

- Avoid risky behavior:
  - *Do not drink (if you are underage) or drink excessively, use illegal drugs, break the law (including traffic violations), get tattoos or body piercings, bounce checks or get into financial trouble, have unprotected sex, etc.* All of these behaviors could lead to issues which will hinder your ability to enlist.
- Instead form healthy habits:
  - *Volunteer. Take up a hobby or a new sport. Get a part-time job. Take a class on a subject which interests you. Learn a new language. Stay current on the news.* All of these will keep your mind and body active and healthy, which will ultimately make you a better candidate for military enlistment.

Talking to Military Recruiters

Recruiters are active duty military personnel who are specially trained to select the young men and women who will join the branches of the service. They are your point of entry into the military, in general, and the Army, specifically. To put it simply, it is their job to decide if you are a good fit for the Army and if the Army is a good fit for you. Their advice can help you make the best decisions for your future. As has been mentioned before, you'll want to make sure that you meet with recruiters from all the branches of the service. An Army recruiter can only answer questions accurately about the Army and as each branch has something different to offer, it is in your best interest to meet with them all in order to get the most information on your options.

Meeting Your Recruiter

There are several ways in which you might meet an Army recruiter. If you take the Armed Services Vocational Aptitude Battery test (ASVAB) in high school, then your scores are usually shared with local recruiters. Assuming your scores are high enough to qualify for enlistment, recruiters will contact you, usually by phone. Calling your local Army recruiting station is a good option. The easiest way to do this is to go to www.goarmy.com and find the nearest recruiter using "Locate a Recruiter." Also on the Army's recruiting site, you can find numbers to call the Army, you can email them to ask more questions, or you can request an information packet. In addition to online contacts, you may meet a recruiter

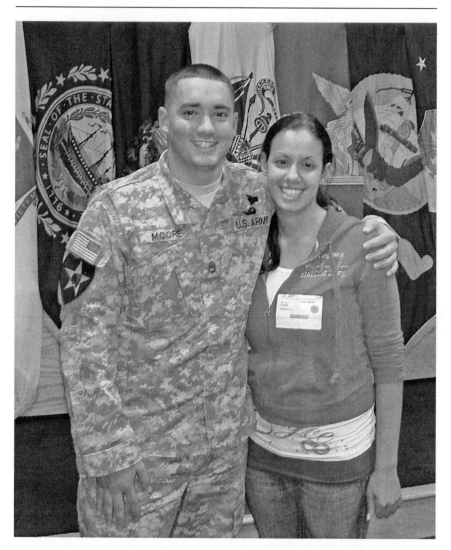

There are lots of places you can meet your recruiter. This future soldier met hers at family dinners — he's her brother! (U.S. Army).

at a community event. Recruiters are often out in the community and in schools, looking for likely candidates for military service.

However you meet your recruiter, you want to be sure that you are comfortable with him or her. The recruiter is going to be your entry point into the Army and you need to be able to trust that he or she has your best interests in mind. The vast majority of recruiters are loyal, hardworking, honest, professional men and women who want to make sure that they are adding the best of the best to the Army. They will tell you the truth and expect it from you in turn. Recruiters are trained in persuasion, much like salesmen, but they are also trained to act as your representative as you navigate the enlistment process. They do not work off of quotas, though they do have goals to meet each year. But those goals are often easily achieved and recruiters then have the luxury of being picky about the new enlistees they sign up.

However, there are a few recruiters who may not be completely aboveboard. If you ever feel uncomfortable about a recruiter for any reason, then you should stop working with them immediately. Look for another recruiter in the same branch of the service, but in a different office and explain — politely and calmly — why you have concerns about the first recruiter you spoke to. Your concerns will be taken seriously and looked into, especially if you are respectful about how you present them. If you are not comfortable speaking with another recruiter, because of anything that the first recruiter may have said or done, contact Army Recruiting Command (contact information is in the back of this book, under "For More Information").

Additionally, if you don't feel that you are completely "clicking" with your recruiter, speak to the other recruiters working in the same office. Personalities vary and you may find a better rapport with another recruiter.

Initial Meeting with a Recruiter

Once you have made contact with an Army recruiter, he or she will ask you to come in for an initial interview. This will give you a chance to learn more about what the Army has to offer you and for the recruiter to learn more about you, so that he or she can make sure you are qualified to enlist in the Army. That initial meeting with your recruiter is a job interview, so you should treat it as such and take it seriously. Here are some important tips:

- Before going into the meeting, do some basic research on the Army so that you will know more about its mission, history, careers, etc.
- Make an appointment and keep it. If an emergency comes up and you need to reschedule, call the recruiter immediately.
- Leave early enough so that you will not be late to the meeting. Don't forget to account for traffic and time to find a parking spot. Some recruiting offices can be tricky to locate, so you might want to get directions online or from the recruiter.
- Dress nicely — dress shirt, slacks, and possibly a tie for young men; a modest dress or a skirt or slacks with a blouse for young women.
- Turn off your cellphone or leave it in the car. Same for MP3 players.
- Shake hands, greet the recruiter by name and rank, and thank him or her for taking the time to meet with you.
- Be an active listener. Listen to everything the recruiter says and be sure to ask for clarification of any details you don't understand. Ask questions and listen carefully to the answers. Don't be afraid to ask "stupid" questions.
- Be open and honest. The military will do background checks on you, so you might as well tell the truth from the beginning.
- Be professional and respectful. You are interviewing the Army at the same time that the Army is interviewing you. Treat this as you would any job interview. If you've never interviewed before, look for some books on interviewing at the library or for interview tips online.

The recruiter will tell you if there is anything specific he or she needs you to bring with you, but you should always bring your:

- Driver's license
- Social Security card

- Birth certificate
- High school diploma
- College transcript (if applicable)
- Permanent resident alien (green) card (if applicable)

There are other items that are a good idea to bring with you. These will save both you and the recruiter time and will help you make sure you have all the information you need:

- A pen and a pad of paper for taking notes.
- Your parents or legal guardians.
  - ○ They will have questions too and many recruiters prefer that they be a part of the initial interview process. If you do not wish to include them or if you are not in contact with them, then you can bring a mature friend or a trusted adult. They are there to help you remember what is discussed. But know that the recruiter needs to ask personal questions about past drug use, medical issues, and more, so be sure that you are okay with talking openly in front of the person who accompanies you.
  - ○ Note: If you are 17, then your parents must come with you and their approval is required for you to be able to enlist.
- Your spouse.
  - ○ If you are married, your husband or wife should come with you. If you have children, though, they should stay with a baby-sitter so that you can have uninterrupted time to talk with the recruiter.
- Your résumé listing any jobs you've held since you were 16.
  - ○ Also bring the names of your supervisors and the addresses and phone numbers of your past and present jobs.
- Medical information.
  - ○ Bring what you know, but you will need to give the military a complete profile during the enlistment process, so the more information you can gather beforehand, the better.

- Information about any law violations, even minor ones like traffic tickets and even ones where your juvenile record was sealed.
- Names and phone numbers for several personal references, people who can speak to your character and personality.
    - These should not be family members. Make sure they have agreed to speak to any recruiters who call them.
- Goals you would like to accomplish in your life.
    - If the recruiter knows what you want to do, then he or she can help you see how the military might be able to help you meet those goals.

You should also bring any questions you have for the recruiter. These can be anything you want to know about the Army, the enlistment process, basic training, military service, etc. Think about these carefully and then type them out on a computer, so that you can easily read them. Again, don't be afraid to ask questions you think are dumb. The recruiter wants to answer all your questions and it's almost a guarantee that he or she has heard every question you could think to ask. Some possible questions:

- Can you explain the enlistment process to me from beginning to end?
- How does the Army differ from all other branches of the service?
    - You should know the basic answer to this from your research, but this will give the recruiter an opportunity to fill in any blanks.
- What do you like about being a soldier? What do you dislike? Why did you become a soldier?
- Can I speak with people whom you have recruited into the Army, both recently and in the past, so that I can find out more about their experiences in the Army?
    - Current service members are excellent sources of information. Remember to speak to them as politely and respectfully as you do the recruiter. Ask them about their experiences during the enlistment process, basic training, follow-on

schooling, and in their first assignments. Ask them if they are enjoying their work and if they plan on re-enlisting. Ask them what their impressions of your recruiter were.

- For potential enlistees who are female: Are there female soldiers I could speak with about their experiences?
    - They will be able to tell you what it is like to be a woman in the Army. Be sure to talk to both new female soldiers and ones who have served for some time. They will give you different perspectives.
- For potential enlistees who are homosexual or bisexual: Are there gay soldiers I could speak with about their experiences?
    - This request will probably be harder for your recruiter to fulfill, since gay service members have not been serving openly before 2011. Ask them about the experience of transitioning from serving under "Don't Ask, Don't Tell," about the experience of serving openly, and about any problems or issues they've face because of their sexual orientation.
- Can I visit an Army base or a reserve unit?
    - If you live near a base or a reserve unit this is a great way to see the Army in action before you enlist.
- What are the job possibilities available to me in the Army? What job did you do before you became a recruiter? Why did you pick that job? What did you enjoy about it? What didn't you like about it?
- How long are enlistment contracts for? How many years will I still obligated to the military after I finish my time in active duty?
    - Even after you finish your active duty commitment, you will still owe the military several years in the inactive reserves, where you can be called back up if needed.
- What rank will I be after basic training? Am I qualified to enter the service at an advanced rank?
    - This usually requires college credit, receiving Eagle Scout or the Girl Scout's Gold Award, several years' participation in JROTC, or a longer enlistment contract.

- How do promotions work in the Army? How often will I be promoted?
- Does the Army offer opportunities to move from enlisted to officer if I so choose?
- How do I choose my job in the Army? Is my career field guaranteed after I finish basic training? Does my chosen job have a comparable civilian job?
- How will I be trained after basic training? What is job training like in the Army — mostly classroom settings or more hands on (or does it depend on the job)?
- How am I assigned to my first duty station? How often will I have to move?
- What is the likelihood I will be sent to war or deployed overseas?
  - This varies depending on the branch of the service. The Army is a ground combat service, so the likelihood of its members being sent to war is high.
- How often will I travel as part of my job?
- What is basic pay? What supplemental pay and allowances are offered? What will I be required to cover from my paycheck (uniforms, etc.)?
- What education benefits does the Army offer? What strings are attached to any education benefits? How does the GI Bill work?
- What are benefits for spouses and families? What is life like on base? What type of housing will be assigned to my family?
- What enlistment bonuses are available? What are the requirements and the restrictions?
  - The Army offers the largest number of enlistment bonuses of all of the branches of the military and upwards of 65 percent of all new recruits receive an enlistment bonus. However, enlistment bonuses often come with strings attached: longer contracts, limited job selection, higher ASVAB scores, etc. You should never enlist solely to get a bonus. Your recruiter will have the most up-to-date information on bonuses.
- How do I make sure that what I sign up for (jobs, bonuses,

benefits, rank, etc.) is what I actually get? What information is on my enlistment contract?

- What retirement plan is guaranteed for career soldiers? How many years do I need to put in? Will I still have health care when I retire?
- What is Army basic training like?
  - o This is covered in Part Four but your recruiter will have the most up-to-date information.
- Am I in good enough shape for basic training? If not, what would I need to do to improve?
- Can I contact my family during basic training?
- What happens if I get hurt or sick while I'm at basic training? What happens if I am unable to complete basic training for any reason?
- What programs do you offer during the Delayed Entry Program to help me prepare for basic training and military service?
- Can I come to the meetings and training sessions you have with new enlistees who are in the Delayed Entry Program?
  - o This will give you a chance to see how the Army helps new enlistees prepare. You will also be able to get a feel for the culture of the Army.
- Can I change my mind about joining the Army while I am in the Delayed Entry Program?
  - o As long as you have not taken the final Oath of Enlistment — which you take just before leaving for basic training — you are able to change your mind. Once you take the Oath, however, you are obligated to follow through on your contract.
- If I leave the Army after my initial enlistment period, what services are available to help me transition back into civilian life? What happens to me if I have to leave before my enlistment contract is up?

These questions, asked during your initial meeting with your recruiter, will allow you to learn more about the Army, but the Army will also want to know more about you. You will fill out a non-binding application, which will give the recruiter the information he or she needs to see if you are tentatively qualified to enlist. You may also, at the recruiter's suggestion, take a mini version of the ASVAB in the recruiter's office. It will give you your basic score (which will tell you if you may be eligible for enlistment) and will let you know approximately how well you'll do on the full ASVAB test. (More on the ASVAB test in Chapter 13.) But you should *not* schedule any other testing at this time. The full ASVAB and your physical can wait until you are certain that you want to join the military and until you know which branch you want to enter.

The most important thing to remember about your initial meeting (and any follow-up meetings) is to listen actively. That means pay close attention to what the recruiter is saying and ask questions to further clarify. Do not let your mind wander. Do not get caught up in the

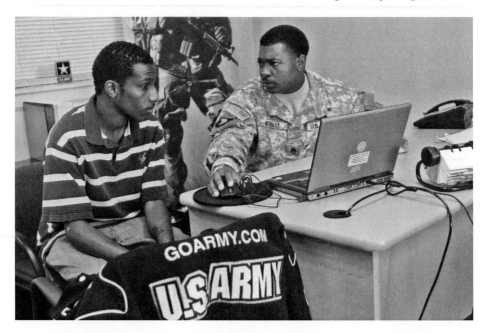

You should listen carefully during your meetings with a recruiter (Official U.S. Army photograph by Sgt. Carl N. Hudson).

excitement of dreaming of a star-spangled military career. There is time for that later. Now is when you need to be objective. Listen closely, ask questions for more information or to clarify, and take careful notes on what you hear. This is very important as you will need those notes later to compare the different military branches.

Second Meeting with a Recruiter

Take the information you learn during the initial meeting and think carefully about it for several days. Discuss the meeting with your parents or with the person who accompanied you. Consider whether the recruiter answered all of the questions you asked. Write down any new questions that occur to you. Compare what you've learned about the Army with what you learned during your meetings with the other branches of the service. This will help you see which branch will be the best fit for your goals and your personality.

The recruiter should, as you are leaving the initial meeting, schedule a follow-up meeting with you. If he or she does not, then request one. It should take place a few weeks after your initial meeting. The second meeting will be the time for you ask any final questions before you decide if you are going to choose the Army, if you are going to choose another branch of the service, or if you are going to choose not to enlist at this time or at all. The second meeting doesn't have to be as long. Take the time to ask any follow-up questions and then thank the recruiter for his or her time. Tell him or her that you will get back to them in a few days to let them know your decision. By this point, you should have met with recruiters from all branches so that you can make a fully informed decision.

Making Your Decision

If you decide that you would rather join a different branch, politely tell your recruiter that you have decided that branch will be a better fit for you. He or she might ask why you decided that the Army was not for you. You can tell them if you like, remembering to be respectful. He or she may also try to convince you to give the Army another look, but should ultimately wish you well. Do not allow any friendly (or non-friendly) feelings for a particular recruiter to change your mind. Your decision should be based solely on the research you have done and comparison between the branches to see which one best matches your goals and your personality.

If after your research, you ultimately decide that military service is not for you, thank your recruiter for taking the time to speak with you. Be polite, but firm, and tell him or her that you are not interested at this time. Tell him or her why you are putting off military service at this time. Your recruiter might have a suggestion for how you can serve anyway, if you so desire. For example, if you prefer to go to college full-time, then your recruiter might suggest you consider the reserves or apply for an ROTC scholarship. If you simply cannot or do not want to join at this time, but you think you might be interested at a later date, then you can tell him or her that you will get back in touch. However, if you think you will not ever want to join the military, say so. Recruiters want to hear the truth from you.

If you decide you do want to enlist in the military and the Army is the branch for you, then your recruiter will start the process of making sure you are fully qualified to enlist in the Army. You are not guaranteed entry into the Army or any other branch of the service. Your recruiter may agree that you are provisionally qualified for enlistment, but there are a number of physical, mental, and moral factors that have to be looked at before you can be completely cleared for enlistment.

The Qualification Process

After you decide that you definitely want to enlist in the Army, the next step is to fill out an enlistment application. This is a form which will follow you throughout the enlistment process all the way to basic training and will be the basis for getting approval to enlist and for your enlistment contract. That means everything on this form needs to be accurate, so read it slowly and carefully, asking questions about any sections you do not understand. Your recruiter will make sure that the information is filled out properly.

The most important thing to remember about the enlistment process is DO NOT LIE. Lying in order to enlist in the military is a felony and when — not if — the military discovers the lie, you will be prosecuted and discharged. You *must* answer all questions truthfully and you *must* provide information to the best of your ability. You will fill out forms to disclose every detail of your medical, legal, financial, and educational history. You must tell the truth about:

- Any past drug use (prescription or illegal)
- Any medical problems that were diagnosed and treated by a doctor (as opposed to ones you only suspect you might have, such as undiagnosed asthma or a "trick" knee)
- Any troubles with the law (even minor ones such as traffic violations and even ones where your juvenile record was sealed or expunged)
- Any pending legal actions (such as being a witness in a court trial or currently going through a divorce)
- Any financial issues (such as bankruptcy or bounced checks)

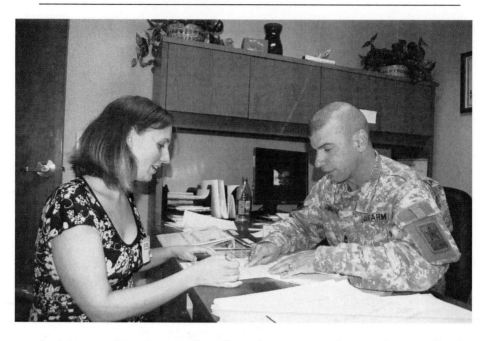

An Army recruiter goes over the enlistment contract with an applicant (Official U.S. Army photograph by Deborah Smith).

Not only should you never lie, but your recruiter should never ask you to lie or to omit information. If your recruiter asks you to change any information, if he or she tells you to leave something off of a form, or if he or she tells you to lie about any aspect of your history, then stop the enlistment process *immediately*. End all contact with that recruiter and report him or her to the Army Recruiting Command. (That contact information is located in the "For More Information" section in the back of the book.)

Depending on your history, you might have some difficulty gathering all the required information. If you've lived and worked and gone to school in one town your whole life, you'll have an easier time finding the needed paperwork than if you've moved around your entire life. But your recruiter can help you hunt down missing information, and by talking to family members, school teachers and counselors, your doctor, and other professionals in your life you should be able to find everything. The more data you collect before you first meet with a recruiter, the less time will be spent searching for it after you make the decision to enlist.

Once you have filled out all of the required forms, your recruiter and other military personnel will go over them. They will be able to tell if you are qualified enough to continue in the enlistment process. There are some issues which will stop the process instantly. For example, if medical personnel at a local Military Entrance Processing Station (MEPS — the location where you go for your physical and to take the ASVAB) look at your medical questionnaire and determine that you have a serious medical issue which will not allow you to pass the required physical, then you will not be allowed to continue in the enlistment process. Unfortunately, there is almost no way to get around such a problem and you will not be allowed to join the military.

Some issues will render you ineligible, but might be able to be resolved with a waiver. Whether or not something can be waived is up to the main recruiting office, not your individual recruiter, though he or she can tell you if something definitely cannot be waived. Waivers take a lot of paperwork and you are more likely to get one if you have only minor issues needing to be waived, rather than if you have major problems. For example, if you smoked pot once three years ago and have never done any other drugs at any time, plus you have an application which otherwise qualifies you, then you are more likely to be approved for a waiver than if you have used drugs more regularly and have other problems which would delay the qualification process.

In addition to revealing any negatives from your past, you should also remember to detail any positives. The Army does allow you to enlist at a higher rank (E-2 or even E-3, rather than E-1) if you have done several successful years of military programs such as JROTC, ROTC, or other military program; if you are an Eagle Scout in the Boy Scouts or have received the Girl Scout's Gold Award; or if you have completed 24 or more semester hours towards a college degree. Your education background can help your recruiter as he or she is helping you pick your job, especially if you already have advanced training or a degree in a specialized area, such as mechanics, computers, music, etc. And volunteer work and other such initiatives show that you are a hard-working person who would be an excellent addition to the Army.

After your recruiter has made sure your enlistment application is completely filled out, that all of the information is accurate, and that you do not need any waivers in order to continue the enlistment process (or that you have received the waivers needed to continue), then you are ready to visit MEPS for your physical and to take the ASVAB.

Visiting the Military Entrance Processing Station (MEPS)

Military Entrance Processing Stations (MEPS) are Department of Defense facilities which exist to help evaluate and process potential military enlistees. They are located in almost every state, as well as Puerto Rico, and both civilians and members from every branch of the military work there. Thousands of applicants a year go through MEPS — getting physicals, taking the Armed Services Vocational Aptitude Battery (ASVAB) test, selecting military jobs, signing enlistment contracts, taking the Oath of Enlistment, and leaving for basic training.

Most enlistees will visit MEPS at least twice. The first time is for processing and evaluation of your physical and mental eligibility for enlistment. The second time is for final swearing in and departure for basic training. But everyone's circumstances vary and your MEPS experience will be shaped by any snags in your qualifications, by how far you live from a MEPS facility, by your type of enlistment (active duty or reserve), or by the branch in which you are enlisting. This chapter will give you the basic information on what to expect at MEPS so that you will be better prepared for your visit or visits.

Staying Overnight

Your recruiter will schedule your visit to MEPS after you have completed the initial qualification process discussed in Chapter 11.

Because he or she wants to be sure that you are on time and ready for your day or days at MEPS, generally you will be required to stay overnight the evening before at a hotel near your MEPS location. Your recruiter will make arrangements for your travel and lodging. Your food and hotel stay will be covered by the government, but it is important that you continue to behave professionally and maturely. At this time you are still being considered as an applicant for military service and any mistakes in judgment are likely to end your enlistment process immediately.

While you are at the hotel, you should:

- *Be respectful of your fellow applicants.* You will be sharing a room with at least one other applicant and you will not have a say in who your roommate is. Be polite and courteous and remember that much of military life is learning to work with those who are assigned to your team.
- *Be respectful of the other patrons of the hotel.* Do not make too much noise talking, watching TV, or playing music.
- *Be respectful of the military and the government.* They are covering the cost of your hotel room, but you will be liable for any additional charges. Do not make long distance calls or charge movies or internet service to the room. Remember to listen carefully to the instructions of the military liaison that is in charge of the applicants staying at the hotel. He or she is responsible for making sure that you know the rules and that you get to MEPS on time.
- *Get to sleep early.* Days at MEPS begin early and your wakeup call at the hotel will be as early as 4:30 A.M. Don't stay up too late or you will not be ready for the long day ahead of you. If you're worried that you won't be able to sleep in the unfamiliar environment, you might try sleeping with earplugs in. They can help block strange noises which might keep you awake.
- *Relax.* This is especially important if you are going to be taking the ASVAB the next day. Don't spend time cramming for the

test. It's more important that you rest up so that your brain is fresh for the test. (More on taking the ASVAB in Chapter 13.)

The military liaison will tell you the wakeup time. You will not have a lot of time to get ready (good practice for when you're in basic training!), so you might want to shower the night before. You should wear comfortable, neat clothing. You don't have to dress up, but you should look professional. A good suggestion is "business casual"—slacks and a nice shirt with closed toe shoes and socks. Do not wear hats, clothes with profane or obscene language and images, or jewelry/body piercings. (You'll just have to take any jewelry off for the medical examination anyway, so you might as well leave it at home where it will be safe.) You must wear underwear, including a bra for women.

Arriving at MEPS

After you are ready and you have eaten breakfast, you will be transported to MEPS for processing. It is important that you remember to bring everything with you that you will need, as you will not be able to return to the hotel to retrieve forgotten items.

Items to bring with you to MEPS include:

- Social Security card
- Birth certificate
- Driver's license
- Permanent resident alien (green) card, if applicable
- Eyeglasses and/or contacts and your prescription, if applicable
- Your medical history (your recruiter will help you get this together)
- Pen and paper, in case you wish to take notes on anything
- A book or magazine to read (you are NOT allowed to bring electronic devices, including cellphones, handheld games, MP3 players, etc.)
- Any other paperwork that your recruiter tells you to take

When you get to MEPS, you will pass through the metal detector and then you will begin the processing. Much of the visit to MEPS follows the old military adage of "hurry up and wait," so remember to be patient and to listen carefully to what MEPS personnel tell you to do.

The first visit to MEPS will usually include the following steps:

- Taking the ASVAB (unless you have already taken it within the past two years)
- Getting a complete physical, including blood work
- Talking to a representative from your branch about career opportunities
- Signing your enlistment contract
- Taking the Oath of Enlistment to enter the Delayed Entry Program (DEP); more on DEP in Chapter 14

It is important to pay attention to instructions while you are at the Military Entrance Processing Station (Official U.S. Army photograph by D. Myles Cullen).

If you have not yet taken the ASVAB, or if you need to retake it for some reason, then that will usually be the first thing you do at MEPS. Some enlistees will take the ASVAB on the afternoon of the first day and then return to MEPS the next day for the rest of their processing. Others will take the ASVAB first thing in the morning and then finish their processing that day. That leads to a very long, very stressful day, though, so it is best to avoid that if you can. Your recruiter will be able to tell you what your options are for taking the ASVAB during your MEPS visit. Chapter 13 tells all about the ASVAB test and the various ways in which it can be taken.

Medical Examination

Whether or not you have taken the ASVAB previously, you will definitely be getting your physical done while at MEPS. MEPS medical personnel will have already looked over your medical files, before you even arrive. The medical information you provided on your enlistment application was sent to MEPS for an initial pre-screening. This pre-screening allows MEPS personnel to rule out applicants who have obvious, major problems. It also gives them a chance to let your recruiter know if more information is needed about a medical issue from your past. That allows the recruiter to work with you to gather that information, so you can bring it with you when you visit MEPS. Then MEPS medical personnel will consider both that information and the information they gather via your medical exam to decide if you are qualified for enlistment, if you need a waiver in order to qualify, or if you are not qualified.

The doctors and nurses at MEPS are not tied to any particular branch of the military and they see potential enlistees from all five branches. Their job is to make sure that you are medically fit for military service. They are not trying to weed anyone out for personal reasons or because they are vindictive and they are not being overly picky about problems that may seem minor to you. They must consider the effect that a seemingly minor medical condition could have on a military unit during battle. They do not want to jeopardize the lives of military personnel by sending someone into battle who will not be able to hold up under fire. They also do not want to put you at risk by sending you for training with a medical issue which will lead you getting hurt or killed.

In order to get a full picture of your medical history and your current physical condition, the staff at MEPS give you a complete physical. This includes:

- Height and weight measurements — including a body-fat measurement if you exceed the weight requirements for your intended service
- Hearing and vision tests
- Range of movement tests — the doctors and nurses will make you stand in a line, wearing only your underwear (males and females are tested separately) and perform a series of movements designed to show problems with your bones, joints, ligaments, tendons, and muscles
- Blood work — for drugs and alcohol, HIV, pregnancy, and general health
- Urinalysis — for drugs and general health
- Medical interview — MEPS personnel will go over the information you provided on your enlistment application and ask you further questions about your medical history. As with the enlistment application, DO NOT LIE
- Specialized tests — if the doctors or nurses decide they are necessary in order to follow up on a suspected issue or problem

There are a lot of medical screenings done each day at MEPS, so during your visit you will spend a lot of time waiting. Remember to be patient and respectful. Bring a book or magazine to keep yourself occupied.

Job Selection

Job selection in the Army is started at your recruiter's office, but the process cannot be finished until you have gone through the MEPS and been qualified for both enlistment and the job you have decided on.

Before you head to MEPS, your recruiter will talk to you about job selection. Recruiters use a program called the Future Soldier Remote Reservation system, which tells them, up-to-the-minute, which jobs are open and which you are qualified for, based on your ASVAB scores (or based on the scores you are likely to get, as determined by the mini version of the ASVAB taking in your recruiter's office, if you haven't taken the full test yet), what you are personally interested in doing, your ability to get needed security clearance(s), your ability to pass physical requirements, etc. By the end of the process, you will have a temporary assignment for the Military Occupation Specialty (MOS)—aka job—you want. That assignment will tell the Army when you need to leave for basic training, based on when your school for your MOS will begin.

Before you meet with your recruiter to discuss the MOSs open to you, you should have a good idea of the types of jobs you are interested in. The basic Army jobs are outlined in Chapter 7, but your recruiter can give you more details about specific jobs within each category. Keep an open mind about your job options. Your ASVAB scores may reveal that you have an aptitude for a career field you hadn't previously considered.

You don't have to pick a job on your first meeting with your recruiter. In fact, he or she should encourage you to think about it for a time. See if you can talk with soldiers who are doing the jobs you are considering. Do they like their jobs? What other jobs would they recommend you look at? The Army does have job services support in place, so if you decide later on in your career (usually after your first term of service) that you'd rather be an infantryman than a helicopter mechanic, you have the option to retake the ASVAB and try to qualify for a new MOS.

After you have completed your physicals at MEPS and taken the ASVAB (if you have not already taken it), then you will head to a meeting with an Army liaison, where you will finish up your job selection and finalize your contract.

Talking with an Army Liaison

In addition to the Department of Defense personnel (doctors, nurses, testing staff, etc.) working at MEPS, there are also representatives from each branch of the service. The Army liaisons at MEPS are there to help you if you need them. While you should have your recruiter's phone number and other contact information with you just in case, the Army liaison will be the first point of contact for any issues you encounter during your visit. He or she can help clear up any problems, fill out paperwork, find needed documents, etc.

The liaison is also the person you will talk to after you complete your medical screening. He or she will go back over *everything* with you again — starting with your enlistment application, going through your medical, educational, and legal histories, and finishing up with any missing information. Though this repetition of information you already organized might seem annoying to you, it is the military's way of making sure that only the best personnel are enlisted. Your talk with the liaison is the chance to make sure that all parts of your application are accurate, so, one more time, DO NOT LIE. Make sure all information is correct and, if not, make sure the corrections are made. The liaison will be making sure you are fingerprinted and that a background check is done, so any discrepancies will be discovered. Finally, the liaison will change your temporary job assignment to a permanent one, after making sure that you are qualified for and still interested in that MOS.

Oath of Enlistment

After you have successfully completed the ASVAB, the medical tests, and the meeting with your Army liaison and all personnel have determined that there are no further issues which will prevent you from enlisting in the Army, then you are ready to take the Oath of Enlistment. This will be the first of two Oaths you take. This Oath of Enlistment installs you into the Delayed Entry Program in an inactive reserve status.

Taking the Oath of Enlistment is the last part of your visit to the Military Entrance Processing Station (DoD Photographer).

The second Oath will be taken the day you leave for basic training and it will install you into the active duty military. (If you are enlisting into the reserves, then you will only take the Oath once. As soon as you take it, you are a member of the military and the reserves.)

The Oath of Enlistment is a serious, solemn occasion. You should not take it lightly. If, after going through processing at MEPS and talking with your recruiter and Army liaison, you have any doubts at all about enlisting, then do not take the Oath. It is better to temporarily disappoint your recruiter than to sign up for something you do not want. Read over the Oath carefully and make sure you are able to agree to it, freely and clearly.

I, _____, do solemnly swear (or affirm) that I will support and defend the Constitution of the United States against all enemies, foreign and domestic; that I will bear true faith and allegiance to the same; and that I will obey the orders of the President of the United States and the orders of the officers appointed over me, according to regulations and the Uniform Code of Military Justice. So help me God.

The Oath is administered at MEPS by military officers. Your family is welcome to attend and to take photographs afterward. If for some reason they cannot attend, MEPS or your recruiter can often stage the Oath at a later time so that they can take pictures then.

After the Oath

After you have sworn the Oath, you will return to the Army liaison to verify your paperwork. He or she will congratulate you on your decision to enlist in the Army and will instruct you on proper behavior during your time in the Delayed Entry Program. Make sure you get his or her contact information, so that you can get in touch with them if needed. Then you can head home.

Your recruiter will receive your paperwork and should call you within a day or two of your return from MEPS. If he or she doesn't call, you should call and schedule a time to go over your paperwork again. Any problems or errors *must* be corrected before you leave for basic training, so it is crucial that you proofread your documents as many times as you can. You will also need to schedule a time to talk with your recruiter about what you can do to prepare for basic training during your time in the Delayed Entry Program. Chapter 15 has some basic tips for how to get ready.

Taking the Armed Services Vocational Aptitude Battery

One of the basic requirements of enlistment is the Armed Services Vocational Aptitude Battery test or the ASVAB. The ASVAB gives the military an idea of what your skills are and what jobs you might be suited for. In this section we'll look at what the ASVAB is, how it is administered, what tests make up the ASVAB, what the scores mean, and how you can work on improving your scores.

What Is the ASVAB?

The ASVAB is basically a test of your knowledge and skills. The military wants to know what you already know about math, science, language, electronics, mechanics, and more, and it wants to know what skills — or aptitude — you have for jobs in various fields. By knowing what you are or might be good at, the military can place you in a job where you can succeed. This is good for both you and the military. If you're successful in your job, then you're more likely to be happy and a happy enlistee is one who is more likely to stay in the military.

To test your knowledge and skills, you take the nine tests that are part of the ASVAB. These tests make up the two parts of the ASVAB: the Armed Forces Qualifying Test (or AFQT) and the technical subtests. Nine tests may sound like a lot, but the individual tests are not long and you do not have to master every one of them. The technical subtests are designed to show the military what skills you have, so that they can match you with a job. The AFQT, however, is the part of the test that will determine whether or not you even qualify to enlist in the military, so it is important that you at least do well on those tests.

How Do You Take the ASVAB?

There are several ways you can take the ASVAB. Many high schools will administer the ASVAB to their students. The students can then use their scores to discuss their aptitudes with their guidance counselor. Since the ASVAB is designed to tell you what you are good at or what you may be good at, it is useful as part of a career decision-making process. If you take the ASVAB at your school, your personal information may be shared with recruiters. They can then contact you to tell you more about the opportunities available to you in the military. If you met your recruiter this way, then he or she can use the scores from the ASVAB you took at school to determine both your eligibility to enter the military and the jobs available to you. ASVAB scores are good for two years, so even if you take the ASVAB in high school, but don't decide to enlist until a year after graduation, your scores are still valid.

However, if you did not take the ASVAB in high school, you will have to take it as part of the enlistment process. At the beginning of your time talking to a recruiter, he or she may give you a mini–ASVAB test (called a Computer Adaptive Screening Test [CAST] or an Enlistment Screening Test [EST]) right in the recruiting office. This test will give both you and your recruiter an idea of how you will probably score on the AFQT portion of the ASVAB. If you do well on that mini-test, then you will likely do well on the full ASVAB. (See the section to come on ASVAB scores for more information on how the test is scored and what your scores mean.)

When you go to take the full ASVAB, you will take it at either a Military Entrance Processing Station (MEPS) or a Mobile Examining Team (MET) site. MEPS is a facility that is run by the Department of

Defense (DOD) to assist and streamline military enlistment for all branches of the service. (See Chapter 12 for more information on MEPS.) MET sites exist solely for the purpose of administering the ASVAB. There are two ways of taking the ASVAB: Computer Adaptive Test (CAT) and Paper and Pencil (PAP). Most MEPS facilities only give the CAT and most MET sites only give the PAP. You are tested on the same type of information, regardless of which type of test you take, but the method of testing is fairly different. Though it is more likely you will take the CAT, you should know how to take both types, because you could end up taking the PAP.

Computer Adaptive Test (CAT)

The CAT is taken on a computer. You will use a mouse to select your answers, though you will have scratch paper provided for working

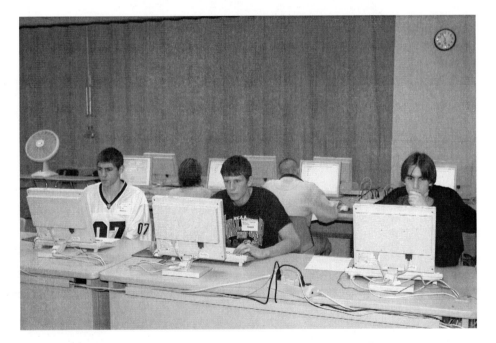

The Computer Adaptive Test is one way you may take the ASVAB (DoD Photographer).

out your answers. But the CAT is not just a computer version of the pencil and paper test. Instead it adapts as you answer questions. The first question for each test will be of medium difficulty. If you get it right, then the second question is a little harder, but if you get the first question wrong, then the next one is easier. You cannot, however, choose the order in which you answer questions in order to answer the easier ones first. You have to take the questions as they are given to you.

The entire CAT takes however long it takes you to finish, though each section has a time limit. Answers are input and then finalized. Once they are finalized, you cannot go back and change them. You keep answering questions until time is up or until you finish the section. Once you finish one section, you move immediately into the next. You cannot go back and check answers on sections you have already finished. You will receive your scores at the end of the test.

Paper and Pencil Test (PAP)

This is a traditional standardized test, using test booklets and bubble sheets you fill in with pencils. The questions vary in difficulty throughout the test. Within a section, you can answer questions in any order you like, which allows you to quickly answer the easier questions and then go back to the harder ones.

Once a section starts you answer questions until you finish or until time is up. If you finish early, you can go back and check your answers and change them if you need to, but you cannot go on to the next section. The PAP test takes about three to four hours. Your scores are mailed to your recruiter within a few days from when you take the test.

How Many Questions Are on the ASVAB?

The number of questions on the ASVAB depends upon whether you take the CAT or the PAP.

#	Name of Test Questions	Type*	CAT # of Questions	CAT Time	PAP # of Questions	PAP Time
1	General Science	Tech	16	8 mins	25	11 mins
2	Arithmetic Reasoning	AFQT	16	39 mins	30	36 mins
3	Word Knowledge	AFQT	16	8 mins	35	11 mins
4	Paragraph Comprehension	AFQT	11	22 mins	15	13 mins
5	Mathematics Knowledge	AFQT	16	20 mins	25	24 mins
6	Electronics Information	Tech	16	8 mins	20	9 mins
7†	Auto Information	Tech	11	7 mins	25	11 mins
	Shop Information		11	6 mins		
8	Mechanical Comprehension	Tech	16	20 mins	25	19 mins
9	Assembling Objects	Tech	16	16 mins	25	15 mins
		Total:	145	154 mins	225	149 mins

Tech = Technical.
†*Auto and Shop Information is two separate tests on the CAT and one combined test on the PAP.*

What Tests Make Up the ASVAB?

ARMED FORCES QUALIFYING TEST (AFQT)

- Arithmetic Reasoning (AR): Basic word problems based on mathematical situations you might encounter every day. Designed to test your ability to reason and solve problems.
- Mathematics Knowledge (MK): General math problems at a high school level, including algebra and geometry. Designed to test your knowledge of mathematics.
- Paragraph Comprehension (PC): You will read paragraphs and answer questions based on what you read. Designed to test your ability to analyze written material.

- Word Knowledge (WK): Questions about the meanings and use of words. Designed to test your vocabulary and communication skills.

TECHNICAL TESTS

- Assembling Objects (AO): You are shown drawings of objects and must answer questions about how they fit together. Designed to test your ability to use spatial reasoning.
- Automotive and Shop Information (AS): Quizzes you on automobile mechanics, tools, shop terminology, uses of parts, etc. Designed to see what you know about mechanics and mechanical work.
- Electronics Information (EI): Questions about circuits, electrical systems, electronics terminology, radio principles, etc. Designed to see what you know about electronics and working with electrical and radio components.
- General Science (GS): Basic science questions — life, physical, earth — at a high school level. Designed to test your knowledge of science.
- Mechanical Comprehension (MC): Tests you on mechanical and physical science principles. Designed to see what you know about how machines work, how mechanics affect real life, etc.

What Do the ASVAB Scores Mean?

There is no overall score on the ASVAB. Instead, there are two separate groups of scores which are important: your AFQT percentile and your composite scores.

THE AFQT PERCENTILE

The AFQT percentile is what determines your eligibility to enlist. It is derived by this formula: 2(VE) + AR + MK. That means that your scores from Paragraph Comprehension (PC) and Word Knowledge

(WK) are combined to create a Verbal Expression score. That score is then added to your Arithmetic Reasoning (AR) and Mathematics Knowledge (MK) scores to give your AFQT raw score. The raw score is compared to the scores of ASVAB test takers who participated in a study in 1997. That comparison allows the test to determine your AFQT percentile. So, if your AFQT percentile is 53, that means that your raw score was better than 53 percent of the test takers in that study.

The military divides the AFQT scores into categories, which are then used to determine a potential enlistee's eligibility. When the military's recruitment goals are lowered (meaning they don't need as many personnel) or when there are more people applying for enlistment than needed, then they usually raise the acceptable AFQT scores for potential enlistees to make sure they are only bringing in the best recruits.

Category	*AFQT Percentiles*	*Category*	*AFQT Percentiles*
Category I	100–93	Category IVA	30–21*
Category II	92–65	Category IVB	20–16*
Category IIIA	64–50	Category IVC	15–10*
Category IIIB	49–31	Category V	9–0†

*Any potential enlistees in Category IV must have a high school diploma, not a GED. Also, only 20 percent of enlistees in the entire military can be from Category IV.

†You are not eligible to enlist in the military if you are in Category V.

Each branch of the military has a different minimum AFQT score. As of September 2010, those were:

Branch	*Minimum AFQT w/HS Diploma*	*Minimum AFQT w/GED*	*Notes about GED Holders*
Air Force	36	65	The Air Force allows less than 1 percent of its yearly enlistees to have GEDs. GED holders who have 15 or more college credits are considered the same as those with high school diplomas.

Branch	Minimum AFQT w/HS Diploma	Minimum AFQT w/GED	Notes about GED Holders
Army	31	50	The Army only allows 15 percent of its yearly enlistees to hold a GED. GED holders who have 15 or more college credits are considered the same as those with high school diplomas.
Coast Guard	45 — and your scores must qualify you for A Schools (training after basic	45 — and your scores must qualify you for A Schools (training after basic)	The Coast Guard has very tight limits on the number of GED holders it accepts. Anyone wanting to enlist in the Coast Guard with a GED must also have completed 15 or more college credits.
Marine Corps	31	50	The Marine Corps allows less than 5 percent of its yearly enlistees to have GEDs. GED holders who have 15 or more college credits are considered the same as those with high school diplomas.
Navy	35	50	Very few GED holders are allowed into the Navy and those that are must not have any issues requiring a waiver. GED holders who have 15 or more college credits are considered the same as those with high school diplomas.

COMPOSITE SCORES

Your composite scores are what determine which jobs you are eligible for. Each branch of the military has a different way of calculating those scores and determining which scores go with which military job. For the current information on how each branch calculates its composite scores and which scores go with which job, visit *http://us military.about.com/od/joiningthemilitary/a/asvabjob.htm* or check out the latest edition of Rod Power's *ASVAB for Dummies* (Wiley Publishing), which has information on which subtests correspond to which military job.

Retaking the ASVAB

If you do not score well enough on the AFQT portion of the ASVAB to qualify for enlistment, you can retake the ASVAB, but not right away. You have to wait thirty days to retake the ASVAB a second time and then wait six months to retake it a third time. Your most recent score is the one which is used to determine your eligibility. Each branch of the military, though, has limits on whether or not you can retake the ASVAB simply to increase your scores in order to qualify for a particular job or enlistment bonus or for a reason other than having an AFQT percentile that is too low for enlistment. Your recruiter can give you the most up-to-date information on his or her branch's restrictions.

The best thing you can do to improve your scores is to brush up on your basic math, science, and vocabulary skills. A high AFQT will open up opportunities for you in the military. You'll be more likely to qualify for waivers (if needed), to qualify for enlistment bonuses, and to qualify for other incentives. Also, because your ASVAB scores remain valid while you are a member of the military, you can use them later on to qualify for advanced training or reclassification into a different job field, though they are not used to determine promotions or awards.

Studying for the ASVAB

Your first step should be go purchase an ASVAB study guide. You can also check them out from the public library or your school or college library, but there may be long waiting lists and you will not be able to write in the library's copy. If you prefer to practice online, check to see if your public library or school or college library has access to an online test prep program. They might and, if so, it will be free to use. Or, to work on your math, science, and language skills, you can use March 2 Success, a free online test preparation program sponsored by the United States Army. You can sign up here: *https://www.march2success.com.* (Using the site does not obligate you to enlist in the Army and they do not share your information with Army recruiters.) March 2 Success does not have a specific ASVAB practice test, but it offers programs to help you boost your basic skills.

Take the sample tests in the study guide or online. They will show you what areas you need improvement in. Then focus your study to those areas. The ASVAB is testing science, math, and vocabulary on a high school level, so if you have been out of school for a time or if you have a subject you were not as good at, then you'll definitely need to brush up your skills.

Though the study guide or online program will have a lot of questions and several sample tests, you should not assume that the questions on the sample tests are the same as those that will be on the actual ASVAB. The ASVAB questions are closely guarded and no study guides — either in print or online — will have access to them. Instead the study guide questions are meant to give you an idea of what type of questions will be on the actual ASVAB and what areas you need to improve in.

Study Tips

- *Be sure to study in a quiet place with good lighting and a firm surface for writing.* Music is okay, if it's not so loud that it distracts you, though you're probably better off sticking with instrumental music, rather than songs with lyrics.

- *Make sure you have all the supplies you need before you begin studying.* Pencils and scratch paper are vital, but you should not have a calculator around to tempt you as you will not be able to use one on the test.
- *Include a stopwatch or a clock so that you can time yourself.* When you take practice tests, you'll want to be sure that you mimic testing conditions, including time limits.
- *Study in longer blocks.* You'll want to set aside an hour or two for each study session. That will allow you the time to focus and absorb information.
- *While occasional study groups can be helpful, make sure you mostly study by yourself.* You won't have anyone to rely on when you take the test, so you need to be sure you can do it on your own.
- *Take notes during your study sessions.* Taking clear notes will help you remember information. Besides, you'll have to take notes in your classes during basic training, so you might as well practice that skill now!
- *Set goals for what you want to accomplish and when.* Your main goal is to do as well as you can on the ASVAB, but also have smaller goals that will help you focus and give you a feeling of accomplishment. Small goals are a good way of breaking your studying into more manageable chunks. You could set a small goal for how much you want to cover in a particular study session or week.
- *Continue practicing even when you aren't studying.* The best way to improve your math and verbal scores is to use your skills all day, every day.
  - *Read the newspaper and a wide variety of books.* Even reading books that are light and fun will help you improve your vocabulary. As you are reading, jot down words you don't know and then look them up in a dictionary. Write down the definition and then make sure to use that word in conversation some time that same day.

121

> o *Use mental math whenever possible.* Rather than reaching for a calculator, do the problem in your head while you're shopping, out to eat, paying bills, etc. Doing quick math problems in your mind or on paper will keep your math skills sharp.

Preparing for the Test

- *Get plenty of sleep the night before.* Don't stay up studying. Last minute cramming will not put the information into your brain and it might interfere with the information you already know.
- *Eat a light breakfast with some protein (eggs, bacon, etc.).* That will help you keep from getting hungry during the test. Have a glass of water to drink, but don't overdo it. You don't want to have to go to the bathroom in the middle of the test.
- *Assemble your supplies the night before.* Your photo ID, pencils and scratch paper are the most important. Bring your glasses, even if you wear contacts. Wear a watch (with a second hand if possible) to help keep track of time.
- *Get to the testing site early.* You'll want to be there at least fifteen minutes before the test starts, so that you can handle any administrative tasks and not feel rushed. Be sure to account for traffic. You might even consider doing a test drive over to the testing facility a day or two before.
- *Reschedule if needed.* If you wake up and feel sick or if you are injured or if you have recently had a stressful event happen, then you won't be at your best to take the test. You can always reschedule. Just call your recruiter and he or she will handle it.

Taking the ASVAB

Your recruiter will arrange the time and location for you to take the ASVAB. He or she will help you work out any transportation issues, such as if you need to stay overnight the evening before the test. If you are taking the ASVAB at MEPS, you may be doing it at the same time as your physical, which can make for a long day or couple of days. But whenever and wherever you take the ASVAB, there are some basic strategies which can help you do better on the test.

DURING THE TEST

- *Relax.* It is just a test. If you are calm, then you will automatically do better on it.
- *Listen to or read all instructions carefully.* If you don't understand, ask the person administering the test to explain.
- *Work steadily, but don't rush.* Getting questions correct is more important than the number of questions you get through. You'll want to answer as many questions as possible, but not at the expense of getting questions wrong.
- *Make sure to read every question carefully.* Be sure that you understand what information is being asked for. Then read all of the answer choices provided to you.
- *Think carefully about what you think the answer is.* Then think about it again.
- *Eliminate logically.* Look at the answer choices. In a multiple choice test, two of them are usually obviously wrong. That leaves two that are possibilities. Choose the one that you think is the best possible answer.
- *If your answer does not match any of the answer choices, then look back over the question.* See if you need to think about things in a different way or look at the answer in a different direction.
- *When in doubt, guess.* As long as you have eliminated some of the answer choices logically, then if you really do not know, make a guess about one of the two remaining choices. You are not penalized for wrong answers; you just don't get a point for them.

Your recruiter is always the best person to ask about the ASVAB. He or she knows the most up-to-date information about the ASVAB and can walk you through the process of studying for it, taking it, and understanding your scores. When you've done the best you can do on the ASVAB, the scores will not only assist you in the enlistment process, but will also reveal more about your career skills. Taking the ASVAB will teach you more about who you are and what careers you might enjoy.

Joining the Delayed Entry Program

Unlike in the past, when you might have gone to MEPS, done your testing and physical, signed your papers, and left for basic training the next day, nowadays almost every person who joins the military enters the Delayed Entry Program (DEP) first. It is extremely rare to leave for basic training any sooner than two weeks after visiting MEPS and most enlistees spend six weeks or more in DEP before departing for training. The military uses the DEP because it allows them to better manage their numbers, spreading out new recruits evenly throughout the year. The branches of the military have set numbers of personnel they have to maintain each year and they need to carefully plan how many personnel are added each week, month, quarter, etc.

The amount of time you spend in the DEP depends on many factors. When your recruiter helps you pick your job, he or she will know when there will be an opening in the school to train you for that job. They count back ten weeks from that date to account for your time in basic training and that gives them the date you will leave for training. That date can be up to 365 days from the time you took the Oath of Enlistment to enter the DEP. And that's good news, because the time you spend in DEP is time you have to prepare for basic training. By getting yourself ready — physically, mentally, educationally, financially — you will set yourself up for success in basic training. The more preparation you have, the better you will do during training.

Behavior in the DEP

Unless you are enlisting in the reserves, you will not be paid during your time in the DEP. (Reserve enlistees can begin attending training sessions with their unit even before attending basic and be paid for their time.) Instead you are a member of the inactive reserves until you ship off to basic. Even though you are not being paid, you still have work to do and expectations you must live up to. Your recruiter and the Army liaison at MEPS will brief you on those expectations, but it doesn't hurt to go over them here as well.

- *Behave like a soldier.* Your time as a "future soldier" (as the Army will refer to you) should not be spent partying and slacking off. You are expected to uphold the values of the Army and to carry yourself as a professional soldier.
- *Prepare yourself for recruit training.* In the next chapter we will go over all the ways you can set yourself up for success during basic training.
- *Attending any scheduled meetings.* Army recruiters have a training process called the Future Soldier Training Program (FSTP). Your recruiter will sign you up for it within ten days of taking the initial Oath of Enlistment. During your time in the FSTP, you will take classes that will help you be a strong, healthy soldier, learning about financial readiness, sexual harassment and assault, stress management, suicide prevention, as well as preparing for the physical fitness requirements of basic. Additionally you will take classes that focus on some of the missions of the Army, studying topics like anti-terrorism and human trafficking.
- *Finish school.* If you are still in high school when you enlist, you MUST graduate and you must do so on time. Otherwise you will jeopardize your enlistment and your job assignment.
- *Keep in touch with your recruiter.* Alert him or her to any changes in your situation, from major ones like marriage or legal problems, to minor changes such as changing addresses.

Leaving the DEP

Because you are not a full member of the Army during your time in the DEP, you can change your mind about enlisting and leave the DEP with no serious repercussions. HOWEVER, this is a very serious step and should only be taken in extreme situations. You should not go through the stages of the enlistment process — talking to a recruiter, visiting MEPS, taking the Oath of Enlistment — without sober consideration of the decision you are making. By the time you enter the DEP, you should be certain of your choice and eager to prepare for basic training.

But things can happen during your time as a future soldier which might cause you to have to change your mind about enlisting. A scholarship to college, the death of a family member, pregnancy, trouble with the law, a serious injury — these are all situations which could arise and prevent you from completing your obligation. The first thing you should do is speak with your recruiter and you should do that as soon as you realize there is a problem. Schedule a time to speak privately and inform him or her of your situation calmly and rationally.

You should know that your recruiter will try very hard to keep you from leaving the Army. By this point in the process the Army has spent a lot of time and money getting you approved to enlist. They feel that you will be an asset to the Army and they aren't going to want to lose you. Your recruiter will try to come up with other options to help you out, such as changing your ship date, getting you approved for a college Recruit Officer Training Corps (ROTC) program, etc. But if your reasons are valid and solid and there is no way you can enlist because of your situation, then they will have to approve your request. You may have to write a letter to the Army Recruiting Command outlining your reasons for leaving the DEP. The address is in the "For More Information" section in the back of this book.

If your situation is temporary — an injury or a family emergency, for example — and you still want to enlist in the Army at a later date, then you will likely be able to, though you might need a waiver to do so. Tell your recruiter if you think that might be the case, so that he or she can help you out. But if you are just experiencing "buyer's remorse" and you want to leave the DEP because you no longer want to be a soldier, then you will more than likely not be considered to be a good candidate for enlistment if you change your mind again in the future. So think carefully before making any decision.

Using the DEP to Prepare for Recruit Training

The best thing you can do during your time in the DEP is to prepare to leave for basic training. You can get yourself in the best possible shape, which will make your time in recruit training easier. The next section has information on how you can prepare mentally and physically.

Preparing for Basic Training

All enlistees worry about basic training. They wonder if they'll be able to keep up physically; they stress about being away from friends and family; they aren't sure how they'll cope with being ordered about all day. Unfortunately the only way to know how you're going to do in basic training is to go through it. Everyone's basic training experience is different, so there is no way to prepare for all the fears and stresses and hardships you'll face. But the Delayed Entry Program gives you the time to prepare to face *most* of those fears and stresses and hardships. If you work hard before you leave for basic, then you'll be ready to work hard during basic, which is what will make you a successful recruit.

There are four ways you should prepare yourself for basic training: physically, mentally, socially, and emotionally. Each of these is as important as the others. By working on them all, you'll insure that you have the best possible start to your basic training experience.

Physical Preparation

Because the physical fitness portion of basic training is what worries enlistees the most and because poor physical fitness sets you up for failure during basic training, physical training is the first aspect of preparation you should focus on. If you are in good physical condition when you leave for basic training, you will find yourself with one less worry during your time there. Your recruiter will give you guidelines for how to get yourself in shape for basic training and he or she may even exercise

Many recruiters will have exercise sessions with their future soldiers to help them get in shape for basic training (Official U.S. Army photograph by Mr. Jorge Gomez).

with you, but ultimately you are responsible for your own physical conditioning.

STARTING AN EXERCISE ROUTINE

The first thing you should do before beginning any exercise routine is to consult with your family physician. MEPS should have caught any serious medical problems, but your doctor should still check you out to make sure you are physically ready for an exercise program. A checkup will also help to catch any physical problems which could delay you when you get to basic training. You don't want to get all the way to training and then discover that you aren't in good enough shape to start!

If you can afford to, joining a gym or a YMCA is a good idea. The staff there can help you plan an exercise program which meets your needs, fits your body, and will get you ready in the time you have. But if you cannot afford a gym, you can still prepare on your own. Your recruiter should give you a pocket sized training guide, which will walk you through the process of getting in shape. The Army's guide can also be downloaded here: *http://www.goarmy.com/downloads/physical-training-guide.html.*

You can check your public, school, or college library for books on exercise and look for exercise plans on the internet. If you are still in high school, talk to your gym teacher or ROTC instructor about helping you plan a workout program. Or, if you are no longer in high school, check with a local college to see if they offer a degree in physical education. If so, talk to one of the professors and see if they would consider giving a student extra credit if they plan a training regimen for you.

Important things to remember as you set up an exercise program:

- *Vary your exercises.* Only focusing on running will not help you develop a healthy level of physical fitness. Be sure that you include all three of these activities:
  - Flexibility exercises (which prevent injury): warm-up and cool-down stretches
  - Cardiorespiratory workouts (which increase your heart rate and improve breathing): running (outdoors is best; don't just run on a treadmill), swimming, biking, rollerblading, active sports
  - Muscular strength activities (which help build muscle): sit-ups/crunches, push-ups, pull-ups (or flexed arm hangs for women), working out on exercise machines or with weights
- *Start slowly.* If you fling yourself immediately into a hard training regimen, you will get injured. Injuries, either during the DEP or during basic, will delay your training which could affect your job training placement, thereby affecting your ability to get the job you want. A severe enough injury could even prevent you from becoming a soldier.
- *Be consistent.* Work out three to five times a week for 45 minutes to an hour at a time. Try to work out at the same time each day so that your body gets used to the routine.

- *Be patient.* If you cannot run a mile when you start training, that's okay. That is why you are training. Start by walking, then add in jogging, gradually increasing the amount of jogging and decreasing the amount of walking. Before you know it, you'll be running!
- *Gradually progress.* Add a little on to your workout each week, not so much as to overload your body, but enough to make sure you are consistently challenged.
- *Aim for endurance, not speed.* Though you will have some timed runs during basic training, most of the runs and hikes you will do will focus on endurance. During your preparations you should start out with longer, slower runs. This will allow you to build up the lung and muscle strength to go the distance when needed. As you train, you will find that you are able to add more miles into the same amount of time.
- *Watch your form.* You'll want to learn the correct, Army way of doing sit-ups and push-ups, so that you do not waste your practice. Your recruiter can help you practice.
  - *Push-ups*: Start with your hands under your shoulders, arms straight, feet together or up to 12 inches apart behind you, toes curled under. Lower down until your arms make a 90 degree angle, then push back up until your arms are straight again. Your body should stay in one line while you do a push-up.
  - *Sit-ups*: Lie on your back with your feet flat on the floor, knees bent. Interlace your fingers and place them behind your head. Raise your upper body until the base of your neck is forward of the base of your spine and then lower your body back down until your shoulder blades touch the floor again. You may not lift your rear end off of the floor and your heels must stay in contact with the floor at all times. A friend can hold your feet for you, if needed.
- *Set a goal.* When you get to Army basic training, you will take an initial fitness test (IFT). The IFT tells the Army if you are in shape enough to handle the rigors of basic training. If you

132

don't pass the IFT or if you are overweight, then you will be sent to the Fitness Training Company (FTC) until you are able to pass it or until you reach an acceptable weight. Your time in the FTC *does not* count towards your time in basic training, so your graduation *will* be delayed.

If you train towards the IFT while you in the DEP, then you'll be more likely to pass it. Since you take the IFT early on in basic training, when you will still be suffering from culture shock and under a lot of stress, you want to aim to be able to do more than the IFT requires. That way you will ensure that you are able to easily pass the IFT when you take it in those stressful conditions.

In addition to training for the IFT, though, you should also look ahead to the Army Physical Fitness Test (APFT). You will take the APFT at the end of basic training and you must score at least 150 points on it or you will not graduate. (You will also have to take the APFT at the end of your job training school and score at least 180 points at that time.) The scoring for the APFT varies according to age and gender. As the requirements to pass the fitness tests greatly increase between the IFT and the APFT, your best bet for being fully prepared is to train for the middle, but aim for the APFT if possible.

Here are the IFT requirements, the APFT requirements, and what you should aim for:

Event	IFT minimum— Men	APFT 150 pts–Men (ages 17–21)	APFT 150 pts–Men (ages 22–26)	IFT Training Goal—Men
Run	1 mile run in 8 min. 30 sec.	2 mile run in 16 min. 36 sec.	2 mile run in 17 min. 30 sec.	1.5 mile run in 13 min.
Push-ups (in 2 min.)	13	35	31	30
Sit-ups (in 2 min.)	17	47	43	40

Event	IFT Minimum — Women	APFT 150 pts — Women (ages 17–21)	APFT 150 pts — Women (ages 22–26)	IFT Training Goal — Women
Run	1 mile run in 10 min. 30 sec	2 mile run in 19 min. 32 sec.	2 mile run in 20 min. 36 sec.	1.5 mile run in 15 min.
Push-ups (in 2 min.)	3	13	11	10
Sit-ups (in 2 min.)	17	47	43	40

Currently the Army is in the process of trying out new requirements for the APFT. Your recruiter can give you the most up-to-date information on what those requirements are and how you can best prepare for them.

- *Stay alert to prevent injury.* Pay attention to what your body tells you. Muscle soreness is normal when starting an exercise routine, but if it seems extreme or if you injure yourself, visit your doctor immediately. Minor problems can become major ones if left untreated.
- *Dress the part.* Proper workout attire will help prevent injuries.
    - Wear clothes that are appropriate to the weather. Avoid plastic suits designed to make you sweat, even if you need to lose weight. These will cause you to overheat and get sick.
    - Wear shoes that work for your feet. Good running shoes don't have to be expensive, but they do need to be properly fitted. Go to a store that specializes in running shoes and get the associates there to assist you in finding the right shoes.
- *Work out with a friend.* You are more likely to maintain and succeed in an exercise program if you have someone to support you. Working out with a fellow future soldier, your recruiter, a friend, or a parent is a great way to get in shape and enjoy yourself at the same time.
- *Have fun.* Exercise can be fun if you allow yourself to enjoy it. In

addition to working on the running, sit-ups, and push-ups you'll need to pass the IFT when you get to basic training, treat yourself to a fun exercise once a week. Join a team sport, take a dance or aerobics class, go for a hike or a bike ride, etc. These treats can keep you interested and engaged in your exercise program.

OTHER PHYSICAL PREPARATION

Besides working out, you'll also want to prepare your body in other ways. By leaving for basic training with the healthiest body possible, you'll be less likely to get sick while you're there.

- *Eat right.* If you haven't already been eating a healthy diet, now is the time to start. Your physician can help you learn more about which foods you should be eating and which you should cut back on. You can also visit the Department of Agriculture's healthy eating website *http://www.choosemyplate.gov* for more information.

  There are a few easy changes you can make which will help your transition to the dining facilities at basic training.
  - *Cut out fast food and sodas and cut back on desserts.* You won't have access to them (or only very limited access), so you might as well get used to doing without now.
  - *Learn to eat quickly and quietly.* Try to eat two of your meals a day in just 10–15 minutes each without talking to anyone, which is about what you'll be doing at basic training.
  - *Drink water.* Water is better than anything else you can drink, including milk, juice, or sports drinks. Try to drink at least eight 8-ounce glasses a day.
  - *Eat a balanced meal.* Make sure you include plenty of fruits and vegetables and that you aren't just eating meat and starches (like bread or potatoes).
- *Lose weight sensibly.* Your body fat must be below 20 percent for males or 30 percent for females, depending on your age. Your

recruiter will tell you if you are above those standards. But be sure to lose weight slowly and carefully. No matter how much you need to lose overall, you should never lose more than 1 to 2 pounds per week. Do not go on a crash diet to lose weight, because you will only rebound later and gain the weight back. Instead learn to eat low fat, healthy meals and be sure to exercise (especially aerobic exercise) regularly.

- *Stop smoking and drinking.* You will not be able to smoke or drink while you are in basic training. Quitting now will not only help you during training, it will also improve your health and make sure you are in good shape before you leave. (It should go without saying that you aren't doing illegal drugs and that you aren't drinking or smoking if you are underage.)

- *Change your sleeping habits.* While in basic you will get up very early every day, often as early as 4 or 4:30 A.M., though sometimes earlier than that. Now is the time to learn how. Start going to bed around 9 or 10 P.M. and getting up between 4:30 and 5 A.M.

    If you will be going to basic training in a location that is in a different time zone from you, it is a good idea to start adjusting to that time zone about one or two weeks before you leave. For example, if you are attending basic training at Fort Jackson (which is on Eastern time) and you live in Wyoming (which is on Mountain time), then you are going to want to go to bed between 7 and 8 P.M. (Mountain time) and get up between 2:30 and 3 A.M. (Mountain time).

- *Toughen your feet.* Start walking in boots now and you will be better prepared for walking in them at basic training. You can use hiking boots if you have them or get a pair of military boots from a military surplus store. Just make sure that your boots fit properly and that you do not run in them. (Almost all running in basic training is done in athletic shoes.)

- *Practice proper hygiene.* Basic training means living in close quarters with other people and that means you'll be more likely to get sick, even though the personnel at basic training do their very best to prevent illnesses. If you make it a habit to wash your hands often, especially before eating and after coughing, sneezing or going to the restroom, then you will decrease your chance of illness.

- *Learn to swim.* Though you do not have to know how to swim to join the Army and you are not required to qualify in swimming during basic training, it is always a good idea to learn. Your time in the Army will take you to a variety of locales and you never know when needing swimming skills will come in handy. Additionally, swimming is excellent cardiopulmonary exercise which will get you in shape for basic training.

- *Practice safe sex.* If you get pregnant during your time in the DEP, you will not be allowed to go to basic training. If your wife or girlfriend gets pregnant, then it can also cause complications for you. The Army will not let you leave basic training to attend the birth, and more than likely won't let you leave your follow on training either. You will also have to work out how you are going to help support your child while you are still only a junior enlisted soldier. Additionally, all recruits are tested for sexually transmitted diseases when they arrive at basic. Being diagnosed with one will more than likely get you sent back home.

- *Avoid injuries, body modifications, drug use, etc.* Drive carefully. Don't take silly physical risks. Do not get a new tattoo or body piercing. Do not use illegal drugs and check with your recruiter to be sure that any new prescription drugs will not disqualify you.

Mental/Educational Preparation

FINISHING SCHOOL

If you are still in high school when you enlist in the Army, then the most important thing you can do during the DEP is to finish school. If you do not graduate, then you will not be allowed to leave for basic training. You don't have to make straight As, but you should work hard, study carefully, ask your teachers for help if you need it, and stay out of trouble. If it looks like you might not graduate or if another school related problem, such as a suspension, arises, alert your recruiter immediately.

KEEPING YOUR BRAIN SHARP

A smart soldier is a good soldier. Just as you work out to keep your body healthy, you want to work your mind to keep it healthy. Basic training isn't just about physical education. There is a lot of learning that will take place during your ten weeks and you want to get your mind ready to soak it all in. Here are some tips for brain workouts:

- *Practice taking notes.* There will be classes in classrooms and on the field during basic training and you will be tested on what you learn. You'll want to be able to take effective notes even when you are tired. The public library will have books on note taking or you can check out the resources at *http://www.college-board.com/student/plan/college-success/955.html.*
- *Turn off the TV and reduce computer and videogame time.* You will not have access to a television, computer, or videogames while you are at basic training. Start getting used to that now by making them an occasional treat, rather than an everyday habit. Use the extra time to work out, visit with friends and family, read, or learn military skills in advance.
- *Work on math skills.* If you do not feel that your mathematics skills are where you want them to be, now is the time to work on them. No matter what your job in the Army, you will use math. The public library will have books on math to help you brush up. One easy way to improve is to stop using a calculator and do all math problems in your head or by hand on paper.
- *Read.* The best thing you can do to improve your mind is to read. The Chief of Staff of the Army has a Professional Reading list which was updated in 2011. It can be found at *http://www.history.army.mil/html/books/105/105-1-1/index.html.*

The twenty-six books on the list are divided into three sub-lists: history and heritage, leadership, and critical analysis and the global context. The goal of the lists is to inspire soldiers to want to learn. Soldiers are encouraged to read not only from the Professional Reading list, but any and all books that interest them. The titles on the 2011 Professional Reading List are:

o History and Heritage:
  - *America's First Battles: 1776–1965* edited by Charles E. Heller and William A. Stofft [non-fiction]
  - *April 1865: The Month That Saved America* by Jay Winik [non-fiction]
  - *John M. Schofield and the Politics of Generalship* by Donald B. Connelly [non-fiction]
  - *The Art of War* by Sun Tzu [non-fiction]
  - *Between War and Peace: How America Ends Its Wars* edited by Matthew Moten [non-fiction]
  - *Gates of Fire: An Epic Novel of Thermopylae* by Steven Pressfield [fiction]
  - *The Killer Angels* by Michael Shaara [fiction]
  - *The Last Stand: Custer, Sitting Bull, and the Battle of the Little Bighorn* by Nathaniel Philbrick [non-fiction]
  - *Once an Eagle* by Anton Myrer [fiction]
  - *The Red Badge of Courage* by Stephen Crane [fiction]
  - *This Kind of War: A Study in Unpreparedness* by T. R. Fehrenbach [non-fiction]
  - *We Were Soldiers Once ... and Young* by Harold G. Moore and Joseph L. Galloway [non-fiction]
o Leadership:
  - *Click: The Forces Behind How We Fully Engage with People, Work, and Everything We Do* by Ori and Rom Brafman [non-fiction]
  - *The Defence of Duffer's Drift* by E. D. Swinton [non-fiction]
  - *Managing the Unexpected: Resilient Performance in an*

Age of Uncertainty by Karl E. Weick and Kathleen M. Sutcliffe [non-fiction]
- *Outliers: The Story of Success* by Malcolm Gladwell [non-fiction]
- *The Starfish and the Spider: The Unstoppable Power of Leaderless Organizations* by Ori and Rom Brafman [non-fiction]
- *Switch: How to Change Things When Change Is Hard* by Chip and Dan Heath [non-fiction]
- *War* by Sebastian Junger [non-fiction]

o Critical Analysis and the Global Context
- *The Age of the Unthinkable: Why the New World Disorder Constantly Surprises Us and What We Can Do About It* by Joshua C. Ramo [non-fiction]
- *The Global Achievement Gap: Why Even Our Best Schools Don't Teach the New Survival Skills Our Children Need—and What We Can Do About It* by Tony Wagner [non-fiction]
- *The Lexus and the Olive Tree: Understanding Globalization* by Thomas Friedman [non-fiction]
- *Monsoon: The Indian Ocean and the Future of American Power* by Robert D. Kaplan [non-fiction]
- *On War* by Carl von Clausewitz, edited and translated by Michael Howard and Peter Paret [non-fiction]
- *Soldier's Heart: Reading Literature Through Peace and War at West Point* by Elizabeth D. Samet [non-fiction]
- *The World Is Flat: A Brief History of the Twenty-first Century* by Thomas Friedman [non-fiction]

THINGS TO LEARN IN ADVANCE

You will learn a lot during recruit training; that is what your thirteen weeks there are for—learning. But there are things you can go ahead and start learning before you even leave for recruit training. Learning these things in advance will save you the trouble of having to

learn them while you are tired, sore, and stressed. Some of the things you can learn are specific to the Army and will help you understand more about its culture and values. Other items are general to all branches of the military and will be used by you on a daily basis while you are serving in the Army. All of these things will be taught to you again while you are at recruit training, but learning them now will save you some brainpower in the future.

Information Specific to the Army

Army Birthday. The Army's birthday is June 14, 1775.

Army Chain of Command. The chain of command tells you who reports to whom. The chain starts at the top with the President of the United States and works its way down to the person directly in charge of you. (The members of the Department of Defense are always civilians.) You will be expected to know the chain of command as it applies to you — title, rank (if applicable), and name of each person — but you will not know the names of some personnel until you get to basic training. Below is the Army chain of command listed in order.

- Commander-in-Chief (aka, the President of the United States)
- Secretary of Defense
- Secretary of the Army
- Army Chief of Staff
- Corps Commander
- Division Commander
- Brigade Commander
- Battalion Commander
- Company Commander
- Platoon Leader
- Drill Sergeant
- Recruit

Army's Core Values. Each branch of the military has its own core values. These are the qualities that they feel are most important for their members to focus on. During recruit training these values are studied extensively and during a service member's career they are expected to live up to these qualities.

The Army's core values are "Loyalty, Duty, Respect, Selfless Service, Honor, Integrity, Personal Courage" and they can be remembered by their initials: L.D.R.S.H.I.P. (or "leadership").

- *Loyalty* means to be faithful and loyal to the United States Constitution, the Army, and your fellow soldiers.
- *Duty* means doing what needs to be done, accepting responsibility for your actions and for the actions of those you are in charge of, and finding ways to improve yourself for the good of those around you.
- *Respect* means following the Golden Rule (only doing to other people what you would want them to do to you).
- *Selfless Service* means putting the needs of the United States, the Army, and those who you are in charge of before your own needs.
- *Honor* means living up to the Army values.
- *Integrity* means doing what is right both legally and morally and doing it even when no one is watching.
- *Personal Courage* means bravely facing fear, danger, and hardship.

Army Emblem. The Army Emblem was officially approved on January 29, 1974. Prior to that, there had been an Army Seal, but that was only used to authenticate documents, not for display. The Emblem was created so that the Army would have a proper design for display.

In the center of the Emblem is a Roman cuirass, a piece of armor, which represents strength and defense. Surrounding it are traditional Army weapons: a sword, musket, bayonet, cannon and cannon balls, etc. The Cap of Liberty is balanced on an unsheathed sword with the Army's motto "This We'll Defend" above it, symbolizing the Army's willingness and readiness to defend the United States. (See image in Chapter 5.)

Army History. One of the aspects of Army recruit training is learning about the soldiers in whose footsteps you will follow. You will find out who they were, when they fought, and what their accomplishments were. This is important so that you understand how the Army has evolved into the force it is today. Since you will be tested on this knowledge while you are in basic training, you should read up on the history of the Army before you leave for recruit training. Chapter 6 has a basic overview of the history of the Army and you can find suggestions for books and websites in the "For More Information" section in the back of the book.

The Army Song. The official song of the Army is "The Army Goes Rolling Along." First Lieutenant (later Brigadier General) Edmund L. Gruber originally wrote it in 1908, but John Philip Sousa, the famous military band director, turned it into a march in 1917. The Army adopted it as its song in 1956. The song is played at the end of all Army ceremonies and soldiers are expected to sing along. You can hear clips of the music or download the entire song at *http://www.army.mil/values/song.html.*

Verse:

> *March along, sing our song, with the Army of the free.*
> *Count the brave, count the true, who have fought to victory.*
> *We're the Army and proud of our name!*
> *We're the Army and proudly proclaim:*

First Chorus:

> *First to fight for the right,*
> *And to build the Nation's might,*
> *And the Army goes rolling along.*
> *Proud of all we have done,*
> *Fighting till the battle's won,*
> *And the Army goes rolling along.*

Refrain:

> *Then it's hi! hi! hey!*
> *The Army's on its way.*
> *Count off the cadence loud and strong;*
> *For where'er we go,*
> *You will always know*
> *That the Army goes rolling along.*

Second Chorus:
> Valley Forge, Custer's ranks,
> San Juan Hill and Patton's tanks,
> And the Army went rolling along.
> Minute men, from the start,
> Always fighting from the heart,
> And the Army keeps rolling along.

Refrain:
> (same as above)

Third Chorus:
> (slower, more freely)
> Men in rags, men who froze,
> Still that Army met its foes,
> And the Army went rolling along.
> Faith in God, then we're right,
> And we'll fight with all our might,
> As the Army keeps rolling along.

Refrain:
> Then it's hi! hi! hey!
> The Army's on its way.
> Count off the cadence loud and strong; (two! three!)
> For where'er we go,
> You will always know
> That the Army goes rolling along! (keep it rolling!)
> And the Army goes rolling along!

Army Motto. The Army's motto is "This We'll Defend."

Army Organization. The Army is organized into units, listed from smallest to largest:

- *Squad*: four to ten soldiers with a non-commissioned officer commanding
- *Platoon*: three to four squads with a junior officer commanding
- *Company*: three to four platoons with a captain commanding
- *Battalion*: three to five companies with a senior officer commanding
- *Brigade*: three or more battalions with a senior officer commanding

- *Division*: three brigades with a senior officer commanding
- *Corps*: two to five divisions with a senior officer commanding
- *Field Army*: two to five corps with the Chief of Staff commanding

You can find more information about Army units and how they are organized at *http://www.army.mil/info/organization/unitsandcommands/oud/*.

Army Rank Structure. Rank structure is what tells you the level a military member has reached in the organization. You will be able to tell someone's rank by the markings on their uniform.

Before you leave for training, you should at least learn the rank insignia for the Army, though it is a good idea to go ahead and learn about the rank structures for all branches of the military. During your time in the Army, you will interact with personnel from all five branches, so if you know the insignia for the other military branches as well, then you're ahead of the game.

The enlisted and officer ranks for all five branches of the military are shown on pages 146 and 147.

Soldier's Creed. The Soldier's Creed was written to help soldiers remember their mission, their duties, and their responsibilities. You will learn the creed in basic training and be expected to live by it.

> *I am an American Soldier.*
> *I am a warrior and a member of a team.*
> *I serve the people of the United States, and live the Army Values.*
> *I will always place the mission first.*
> *I will never accept defeat.*
> *I will never quit.*
> *I will never leave a fallen comrade.*
> *I am disciplined, physically and mentally tough, trained and*
> *   proficient in my warrior tasks and drills.*
> *I always maintain my arms, my equipment and myself.*
> *I am an expert and I am a professional.*
> *I stand ready to deploy, engage, and destroy the enemies of the*
> *   United States of America in close combat.*
> *I am a guardian of freedom and the American way of life.*
> *I am an American Soldier.*

RANK INSIGNIA OF THE U.S. ARMED FORCES

ENLISTED

	E-1	E-2	E-3	E-4	E-5	E-6	E-7	E-8	E-9	SENIOR ENLISTED ADVISORS

ARMY

| no insignia | Private E-2 (PV2) | Private First Class (PFC) | Corporal (CPL) / Specialist (SPC) | Sergeant (SGT) | Staff Sergeant (SSG) | Sergeant First Class (SFC) | Master Sergeant (MSG) / First Sergeant (1SG) | Sergeant Major (SGM) / Command Sergeant Major (CSM) | Sergeant Major of the Army (SMA) |
| Private E-1 (PV1) | | | | | | | | | |

MARINES

| no insignia | Private First (PFC) | Lance Corporal (LCpl) | Corporal (Cpl) | Sergeant (Sgt) | Staff Sergeant (SSgt) | Gunnery Sergeant (GySgt) | Master Sergeant (MSgt) / First Sergeant (1stSgt) | Master Gunnery Sergeant (MGySgt) / Sergeant Major (SgtMaj) | Sergeant Major of the Marine Corps (SgtMajMC) |
| Private (Pvt) | | | | | | | | | |

AIR FORCE

| no insignia | Airman (Amn) | Airman First Class (A1C) | Senior Airman (SrA) | Staff Sergeant (SSgt) | Technical Sergeant (TSgt) | Master Sergeant (MSgt) / First Sergeant (E-7) | Senior Master Sergeant (SMSgt) / First Sergeant (E-8) | Chief Master Sergeant (CMSgt) / First Sergeant (E-9) / Command Chief Master Sergeant (CCM) | Chief Master Sergeant of the Air Force (CMSAF) |
| Airman Basic (AB) | | | | | | | | | |

NAVY

| no insignia | Seaman Apprentice (SA) | Seaman (SN) | Petty Officer Third Class (PO3) | Petty Officer Second Class (PO2) | Petty Officer First Class (PO1) | Chief Petty Officer (CPO) | Senior Chief Petty Officer (SCPO) | Master Chief Petty Officer (MCPO) / Force or Fleet Command Master Chief Petty Officer (FORMC) (FLTMC) | Master Chief Petty Officer of the Navy (MCPON) |
| Seaman Recruit (SR) | | | | | | | | | |

COAST GUARD

| Seaman Recruit (SR) | Seaman Apprentice (SA) | Seaman (SN) | Petty Officer Third Class (PO3) | Petty Officer Second Class (PO2) | Petty Officer First Class (PO1) | Chief Petty Officer (CPO) | Senior Chief Petty Officer (SCPO) | Master Chief Petty Officer (MCPO) / Command Master Chief (CMC) | Master Chief Petty Officer of the Coast Guard (MCPO-CG) |

www.army.mil/symbols

146

RANK INSIGNIA OF THE U.S. ARMED FORCES

OFFICERS

O-1	O-2	O-3	O-4	O-5	O-6	O-7	O-8	O-9	O-10	SPECIAL

ARMY - AIR FORCE - MARINES

| Second Lieutenant (2LT) | First Lieutenant (1LT) | Captain (CPT) | Major (MAJ) | Lieutenant Colonel (LTC) | Colonel (COL) | Brigadier General (BG) | Major General (MG) | Lieutenant General (LTG) | General (GEN) | General of the Army (GA) |

NAVY - COAST GUARD

| Ensign (ENS) | Lieutenant Junior Grade (LTJG) | Lieutenant (LT) | Lieutenant Commander (LCDR) | Commander (CDR) | Captain (CAPT) | Rear Admiral Lower Half (RADM)(L) | Rear Admiral Upper Half (RADM)(U) | Vice Admiral (VADM) | Admiral (ADM) | Fleet Admiral (FADM) |

W-1	W-2	W-3	W-4	W-5

ARMY

| Warrant Officer (WO1) | Chief Warrant Officer (CW2) | Chief Warrant Officer (CW3) | Chief Warrant Officer (CW4) | Chief Warrant Officer (CW5) |

NAVY - COAST GUARD

| Warrant Officer 1 W-1 * The grade of Warrant Officer W-1 is no longer in use. | Chief Warrant Officer (CWO2) | Chief Warrant Officer (CWO3) | Chief Warrant Officer (CWO4) | NO Chief Warrant Officer (CWO5) |

MARINES

| Warrant Officer (WO) | Chief Warrant Officer (CWO2) | Chief Warrant Officer (CWO3) | Chief Warrant Officer (CWO4) | Chief Warrant Officer (CWO5) |

AIR FORCE

| NO WARRANT | NO WARRANT | NO WARRANT | NO WARRANT | NO WARRANT |

www.army.mil/symbols

Information General to All Branches of the Military

General Orders of a Sentry. The general orders are what you do when you are standing guard. You will be expected to know — by heart — the general orders. The Coast Guard, Marine Corps, and Navy have eleven general orders, while the Army and Air Force have a condensed, three-item list of orders. Here is the Army version:

1. *I will guard everything within the limits of my post and quit my post only when properly relieved.*
   - You are in charge of the area assigned to you and must remain in charge until the next assigned guard arrives to take over from you.
2. *I will obey my special orders and perform all of my duties in a military manner.*
   - You must follow all instructions given to you when you took charge of your guard post and you must behave professional and responsibly while on duty.
3. *I will report violations of my special orders, emergencies, and anything not covered in my instructions to the commander of the relief.*
   - This means that you must tell your instructor about any and all problems that occur while you are on guard, such as if someone tries to enter without authorization.

Military Alphabet. The branches of the military have a shared phonetic alphabet. A phonetic alphabet is an alphabet where a sound or a word represents a letter. You know how when people spell something over the phone and the letters "b" and "v" or "t" and "p" sound very similar? That's why the military uses the phonetic alphabet instead. "Bravo" and "Victor" sound very different and keep personnel from getting letters confused when communicating. Here is the military phonetic alphabet:

Letter	Phonetic Word	Letter	Phonetic Word
A	Alpha	N	November
B	Bravo	O	Oscar

Letter	Phonetic Word	Letter	Phonetic Word
C	Charlie	P	Papa
D	Delta	Q	Quebec
E	Echo	R	Romeo
F	Foxtrot	S	Sierra
G	Golf	T	Tango
H	Hotel	U	Uniform
I	India	V	Victor
J	Juliet	W	Whiskey
K	Kilo	X	X-Ray
L	Lima (LEE-ma)	Y	Yankee
M	Mike	Z	Zulu

Military Time. Military time is designed to prevent confusion when information is communicated between personnel, just like the military alphabet. Military time is based on twenty-four hours rather than twelve. You do not have to use A.M. or P.M., because all of the hours are different. The word "zero" is used in every spot that doesn't have a number 1–9 and you do not use a colon between the hours and the minutes. So 2:05 A.M. would be Zero two zero five or 0205.

Time	Military Time	Pronunciation
12 A.M.	0000	Zero-zero-zero-zero
1 A.M.	0100	Zero one hundred
2 A.M.	0200	Zero two hundred
3 A.M.	0300	Zero three hundred
4 A.M.	0400	Zero four hundred
5 A.M.	0500	Zero five hundred
6 A.M.	0600	Zero six hundred
7 A.M.	0700	Zero seven hundred
8 A.M.	0800	Zero eight hundred
9 A.M.	0900	Zero nine hundred
10 A.M.	1000	Ten hundred
11 A.M.	1100	Eleven hundred
12 P.M.	1200	Twelve hundred
1 P.M.	1300	Thirteen hundred
2 P.M.	1400	Fourteen hundred
3 P.M.	1500	Fifteen hundred

Time	Military Time	Pronunciation
4 P.M.	1600	Sixteen hundred
5 P.M.	1700	Seventeen hundred
6 P.M.	1800	Eighteen hundred
7 P.M.	1900	Nineteen hundred
8 P.M.	2000	Twenty hundred
9 P.M.	2100	Twenty-one hundred
10 P.M.	2200	Twenty-two hundred
11 P.M.	2300	Twenty-three hundred

Military Terminology. As you can see, the military likes to use its own words and abbreviations. This can be confusing until you get used to it. Your drill instructors will be more than happy to tell you what they want you to call things, but if you get a basic grasp of terms before you leave for training, you'll feel less like you wandered into foreign country. There is a glossary in the back that has basic terms used throughout this book and there are several sources of information online:

- The Department of Defense: *http://www.dtic.mil/doctrine/dod_dictionary*
- TodaysMilitary.com: *http://www.todaysmilitary.com/inside/military-glossary*

Uniform Code of Military Justice. The Uniform Code of Military Justice (UCMJ) is the body of military law. Parts of it spell out what happens to military personnel when they break the law. While you do not need to memorize the UCMJ (it's too long for that), you should read it over. As soon as you take the final Oath of Enlistment and leave for basic training, you are bound by the UCMJ and can be court-martialed for infractions. The parts of the UCMJ can be found here: *http://www.law.cornell.edu/uscode/html/uscode10/usc_sup_01_10_10_A_20_II_30_47.html.*

Your Social Security Number. The Army will need you to fill out many forms, right when you first arrive at basic training, while you're still shell-shocked. Your Social Security number will need to be written on almost all of them, so it is important that you have it memorized before you arrive. It is also a good idea to know just the last four digits of your number as that is often used to identify you while you are in the military.

What You Don't Need to Learn in Advance

One aspect of preparing for recruit training might surprise you — you do not need to learn how to handle a weapon before you leave for training. The Army has a specific way they teach recruits to shoot and they've found that those recruits who enter basic training never having handled a weapon are much more likely to qualify on their first try and to earn marksmanship medals than those recruits who have grown up around guns. That's because recruits who have never fired a weapon don't have to unlearn poor habits, whereas the recruits who are more familiar with firearms don't always listen as carefully to instructions and then make mistakes.

The best way you can prepare for military weapons training is to relax and not worry about it. Your instructors will teach you everything you need to know and as long as you don't stress about it, you will do just fine. If you already know your way around a gun, then your best bet is to forget everything you have learned and go into Army training willing to start learning about weapons from the basics on up. Be open to learning the Army way to shoot and be eager to listen to everything your instructors tell you and you will qualify quickly.

You also do not have to learn how to drill, or march in formation, before you leave. Your instructors do not expect you to know how to drill when you arrive and they will begin showing you the basics as soon as you arrive. If you want to know more about military drill, however, it doesn't hurt to look over the Army Drill and Ceremonies manual, so that you understand the basic terms before you get to training. It can be found on a number of National Guard and JROTC websites, such as: *http://www.gasdf.com/regs/FM_3–21–5_Drill_Ceremonies.pdf.*

Social Preparation

In addition to preparing your mind and body for the basic training experience, you will need to make sure to put your bills and other affairs in order. That way problems will not arise while you are in training and unable to deal with them. Also, you will need to get your friends and family ready for you to be gone.

GETTING YOUR AFFAIRS IN ORDER

There are things you will need to be sure to organize before you leave because you will not be able to take care of them while you are in basic training.

- *Open a bank or credit union account.* If you do not already have an account with a bank or a credit union, you will need to open one. Your recruiter can tell you what credit unions are common to Army bases, if you prefer to have an account at one of them. Otherwise, you can simply choose a bank that is convenient to you at this time. Be sure to get a debit card and to verify that it works before leaving for basic training.
- *Set up direct deposit.* Your recruiter will have the form for you to set up direct deposit of your military pay into your bank or credit union account. NOTE: Military pay can take 30 to 45 days to get started in direct deposit, so it is a good idea to have some money in your account in case of emergencies. One to two hundred dollars will work if you can afford it.
- *Bills.* You will not have access to your bank account, a computer, a check card, etc. while you are in training. Here are some suggestions for handling bills for your house, car, etc.:
  - *Pay off as many as possible.* If you leave for basic training debt free, then you won't have bills hanging over your head after graduation.
  - *Arrange for automatic payments.* Any bills that you cannot

pay off should be set up to be automatically paid from your bank or credit union account.

   o *Have a trustworthy person handle them.* If you are married, this will be your spouse. Otherwise, choose someone who is financially responsible. A drinking buddy or someone you are dating is not a good choice.

- *Car.* If your car or other vehicle is paid off, does not have great sentimental value to you, and is not needed by your family, then you might consider selling it so that you don't have to worry about it while you're gone. Otherwise, arrange for the payment to be made automatically. If you leave it with someone, make sure they are trustworthy and that either your or their insurance will allow them to drive it if that is okay with you. Or you can arrange for it to be kept in storage until after graduation. If your driver's license or vehicle registration will expire while you are gone, see if you can go ahead and renew them before you leave.

- *Cellphone.* Check with your cellphone company to arrange for a military hold on your account. That way you won't have to pay for minutes you aren't using during basic training.

- *Paperwork.* Make sure you have copies of the documents you may need at basic training. These could include your marriage license, divorce paperwork, Social Security card, etc. While you're gone, important papers should be stored in a fireproof safe and the key should be given to a trustworthy family member or friend. If you are married, make sure that you give your spouse power of attorney which will allow them to sign in your name while you are away. Your recruiter can help you get the correct form and fill it out.

- *Legal issues.* You will not be able to leave for basic training with outstanding legal issues. Resolve any legal problems as quickly as possible and avoid getting involved in any new issues, even minor ones such as traffic violations. Keep your recruiter apprised of any legal problems you encounter during the DEP.

GETTING YOUR FAMILY AND FRIENDS
READY FOR YOUR ABSENCE

Leaving family and friends for ten weeks is hard for you, but it will also be hard on them. You can help ease their pain before you leave and they can help support you while you're gone.

- *Encourage them to write to you.* During Army recruit training you will not be able to receive or make phone calls unless your drill sergeant decides to allow you, so mail is very important way for you to stay in contact with your friends and family. You can get mail every day except Sundays and holidays. You will be given time to write home, so ask your friends and family to write to you.

    Letters from home should be upbeat and cheerful. Ask them to help you keep your spirits up by offering words of encouragement. Bad news is sometimes unavoidable, but it helps if family and friends use their letters to you to relay mostly good things that happen. Even simple details of home life can help. They are welcome to send pictures, but care packages are not allowed.

    To help ensure you receive letters, partially address and stamp envelopes to yourself before you leave. You won't find out your recruit training address until you arrive, but you can go ahead and get the supplies together for your family so that they can concentrate on writing you uplifting letters.

- *Help your children understand what you'll be doing.* If you are a parent, then you'll need to prepare your kids for your absence. There are books for younger readers about the Army in the "For More Information" section. Reading these with your child will help him or her understand your new job. You can also watch some of the videos about recruit training listed in that section, so that they can see what you'll be experiencing. Ask your kids to write to you every day and promise that you'll write to them as well.

- *Have a going away party.* This is a great way to enjoy time with friends and family, but there are a few things to keep in mind.
  - *Don't have the party the night before you leave.* You'll want to be rested, not tired from staying up all night. Instead have your get-together the weekend before you leave.
  - *Don't use drugs at the party, do not have unprotected sex, and do not drink if you are underage.* Drugs and alcohol in your system will be discovered upon your arrival at basic training and unprotected sex could lead to pregnancy or a disease. All of these will keep you from completing training.
- *Remind them that you love them and that their support is important to your success.* They probably know it, but it's nice to hear again.

Emotional Preparation

Even if you are entering basic training dreaming of becoming a hardened warrior, you will still want to prepare yourself emotionally for the adventure on which you are about to embark. Begin by psyching yourself up during your time in the DEP.

- *Don't go in thinking that training will be too difficult.* You've prepared yourself during your time in the DEP, so you are ready for recruit training.
- *Enter basic training eager to learn.* Recruit training is all about learning the basics of being a soldier. By the time you leave for training, you should be excited about spending all day every day learning something new. That excitement will carry you through any rough patches.
- *Know that training is planned so as to give you the tools you need.* Every lesson you will learn in recruit training will prepare you for the next lesson. Pay attention and work hard and you *will* learn what you need to learn.
- *Remember that recruit training is not what life in the Army will be*

like every day. Recruit training is only ten weeks long. You *can* get through it and then you will go on to enjoy being a soldier.

- *Believe that you can succeed.* The Army selected you just as much as you selected them. They saw something in you; now you need to see it in yourself. If you want to be a soldier and you work with that goal in mind, then you will succeed.

If you want to give yourself a lift while you are at recruit training, sit down and write yourself ten letters or postcards. In each one, remind yourself why you decided to become a soldier, tell yourself that you are determined to succeed, and offer yourself encouraging words. You can slip in a photograph of a pet or your family or your friends; something that will make you smile when you see it. Stamp the letters or postcards and put a date on the outside of each one — one letter or postcard per week of basic training. Then give the letters to your recruiter, a parent, or a trusted friend and ask them to mail one to you each week while you are at basic training.

As your time in the DEP is drawing to a close, start looking towards the future. Soon you will leave for basic training and your journey to becoming a soldier will begin. To give you an idea of what to expect during those ten weeks, the next chapter will tell you what happens in basic training, from the moment you arrive until the day you proudly graduate.

FOUR

Army
Basic Training

Overview

The goal of basic training, also called recruit training, is to take a civilian and turn him or her into a basic soldier. Basic training is just that — the *basic* knowledge that new military members need to become a part of the Army. Recruits learn how to march, how to use a variety of weapons, how to fight, how to maneuver in a variety of conditions, how to administer first aid, how to read standard navigational aids, how to work as part of a team, as well as learning military and Army history, ethics, etiquette, customs, dress, etc.

Army basic training — called Basic Combat Training or BCT — lasts for nine weeks. Before basic training begins, new recruits go through three to five days of reception, so they are at their training location for ten weeks overall. Every day of the week is a training day, even Sundays and even holidays, though recruits are allowed time for religious activities on Sunday mornings (more information on religious services is in Chapter 20). Recruits spend their days doing physical training, learning military skills (either in the classroom or hands on), and practicing what they've been taught. Training personnel make sure that even mundane activities like cleaning the barracks are an opportunity for learning how to do things the military and Army way.

Army Basic Training Locations

The Army trains recruits at four locations: Fort Jackson in Columbia, South Carolina; Fort Leonard Wood in Waynesville, Missouri; Fort Sill in Lawton, Oklahoma; and Fort Benning in Columbus, Georgia. Where you go often depends on what your job will be. Each BCT location usually has Advanced Individual Training (or AIT) schools. These are the schools you go to after BCT is over. The Army sends you to a BCT location that corresponds with the AIT school you will go to, either at the same base or one that is near to the base where you attended BCT. The locations and their related jobs are:

- Fort Leonard Wood: combat engineers, military police, and chemical warfare
- Fort Benning: infantry and armor [NOTE: because women are not allowed in infantry and armor MOSs, no women attend BCT at Fort Benning]
- Fort Sill: field artillery
- Fort Jackson: all other MOSs (personnel, medical, etc.)

One Station Unit Training

The Army has a unique type of training called One Station Unit Training or OSUT. In OSUT, you move straight from basic combat training (BCT) into job training (Advanced Individual Training, or AIT) without a graduation ceremony in the middle. This option is only for combat arms jobs: infantry, armor, etc. If you attend OSUT, then you will be in training for the ten weeks of BCT and then however many additional weeks your AIT takes. After that you will have your graduation ceremony. This option is available at Fort Benning, Fort Leonard Wood, and Fort Sill.

Drill Sergeants

Drill sergeants are the main training personnel in charge of recruits. Usually each company of recruits has three drill sergeants. The senior drill sergeant oversees all aspects of his or her company's training and acts as a father or mother figure to the recruits, motivating them or challenging them as needed. One of the other two drill sergeants acts

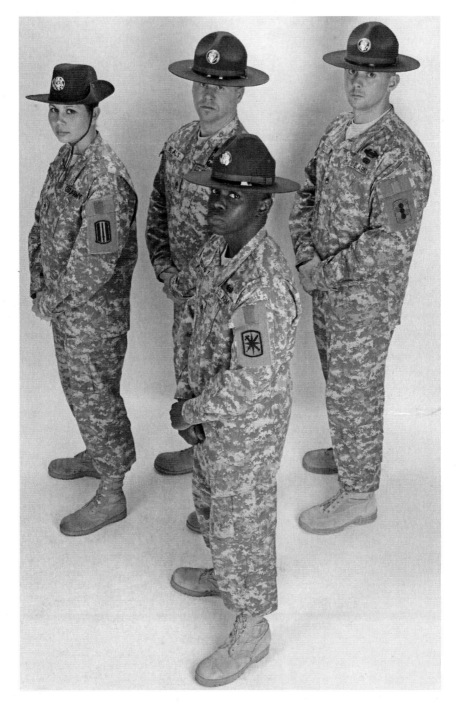

Drill sergeants are easily identified by their distinctive hats and their no-non-sense attitude (Official U.S. Army photograph by Tammy Garner).

as the "bad cop," the hard disciplinarian of the group, and the other is responsible for teaching recruits how to drill, or march in formation.

Drill sergeants are highly trained individuals. They are senior enlisted personnel who must complete an intensive course that recreates every aspect of basic training. During their training, they learn how to motivate, instruct, and discipline. They must memorize all possible drill routines and be completely familiar with the standard operating procedures that drill sergeants must follow.

Soldiers serve as drill sergeants for several years and while they are in charge of a training company they can work upwards of 120 hours a week, on very little sleep and without seeing their families. They know how to do, and have done, everything that they tell recruits to do. When they are not overseeing a training company, many of them work as instructors in different areas of recruit training. Drill Sergeants are the only soldiers who wear the distinctive campaign hat — aka, the "Smokey the Bear" hat.

Gender Integrated Training

The Army trains male and female recruits together in integrated companies, except at Fort Benning. (The Marine Corps is the only branch of the service that trains men and women separately.) Training for males and females is exactly the same, though a few of the female physical requirements are lighter. All recruits may have either male or female Drill Sergeants in charge of them during the day, but at night and in their barracks, female recruits have female Drill Sergeants in charge of them.

Training Schedule

The first few days at basic training you will be at the Reception Battalion. During this time new recruits receive their gear and undergo a series of medical and physical fitness tests to make sure they are ready for basic training. After that they are sent to their designated training company for recruit training.

Army recruit training is divided into three phases. Each week of the phase is related to a different Army core value.

- *Phase One* or *Red Phase*: Week 1 (Introduction), Week 2 (Loyalty), and Week 3 (Duty). During this time recruits begin learning the basics of being in the military and being soldiers. They begin learning hand-to-hand combat and how to operate in the field.
- *Phase Two* or *White Phase*: Week 4 (Respect), Week 5 (Selfless Service), and Week 6 (Honor). During this time recruits learn the basics of marksmanship (or firing their weapons).
- *Phase Three* or *Blue Phase*: Week 7 (Integrity), Week 8 (Personal Courage), and Week 9 (Graduation). During this time recruits learn more about marksmanship and they study maneuvers in the field. Phase Three ends with a final event field training exercise which tests everything the recruits have learned and Graduation.

After graduation, new soldiers leave immediately for further training. You will not get leave until after you finish your training at your AIT school.

Basic Training Tips

Army basic training is designed to break down you as a civilian and remake you into a soldier. But this process cannot happen without your help. That means that in order to succeed in basic training you have to *decide* that you are going to succeed. There are things you can do that will help ensure you have a successful time in basic training.

- *Adjust your attitude.* You might be the best student in your school or the toughest person in your neighborhood, but the moment you set foot in Basic Combat Training you become the lowest rung of the ladder. You have to work your way back up, through each of the phases of training, to show that you can handle the responsibility of being a soldier. High and mighty attitudes and chips on your shoulder have no place in recruit training, not with your drill sergeants and not with your fellow recruits.
- *Accept the loss of freedom.* You will have to do what the military says; there is no way to get around that. Fighting the system will only frustrate you. Instead accept that you are giving up some freedoms and remind yourself of what you are receiving in return. After all, even if you stayed a civilian and got a job in an office or a factory or a store, you would still have to bend to the rules of your organization.
- *Don't take things personally.* Drill sergeants are going to yell, but they don't do it because they hate you. They do this to see how you handle yourself when you are under stress. Combat is stressful and the Army need personnel who can keep going even when tired and harassed. Know that the yelling and the

other stresses are not directed at you personally and know that learning to handle them will make you a stronger person.

- *Don't be lazy and don't give up.* Drill sergeants want recruits who work hard, try their best, and don't quit. Nothing will make them mad faster than laziness or recruits who stop before giving everything they can. If they think you can keep going, then you can. Ignore the voice in your head telling you to stop. Persevere. You'll be surprised by how much you can accomplish.

- *Don't show off.* Just as you don't want to give up too soon, you also don't want to always strive to beat everyone around you. That is not the sign of a good leader or a good teammate and the Army want recruits who can be both. The only person you are competing with is yourself. Be the best *you* can be at everything you are assigned and don't worry about trying to outdo your fellow recruits. Basic training is about what *you* can accomplish. Those recruits who excel and win awards are the ones who aren't trying for acclaim. They are simply doing their very best every single day of training.

- *Do what you are told, when you are told, and how you are told—without question.* In a combat situation there is not time to question orders. Your drill sergeants are preparing you for that now by expecting you to immediately obey every order — no matter how bizarre or impossible — without questioning. The sooner you learn to do this, the easier time you'll have during recruit training.

- *Tell the truth and do not make excuses.* NEVER lie to your drill sergeants for any reason. They will know that you lied and they will make your life harder because of it. If you made a mistake, admit to it, but don't try to explain why. If you don't know the answer, admit to it. Your life will be much easier if you keep things honest and if you don't try to justify your actions.

- *Pay close attention. Pay especially close attention to safety issues.* No matter how tired you are, pay attention to everything your drill sergeants say. Often they will be giving you hints (or even outright telling you) about what you can expect during training or the best way to complete an exercise. Pay even closer attention when they are talking about safety. The military takes safety very seriously, especially during training. Nothing will get you in trouble faster than ignoring or forgetting instructions.

- *Encourage teamwork.* Teamwork is paramount to military life. The Army will expect you to immediately work as a team with your fellow recruits. Your drill sergeants will not care if you don't like someone. In fact, not liking them makes it even more likely that you will be forced to work together! The faster you and your fellow recruits learn to work together — in the field, in the barracks, and in the classroom — the better your basic training experience will be.
- *Look out for your fellow soldiers.* Part of the Soldier Creed is "I will never leave a fallen comrade." This philosophy begins in basic training. Whenever possible, help out your fellow recruits and they, in turn, will help you.
- *Deal with differences maturely.* Your fellow recruits will be from all parts of the country, all types of backgrounds, all ages, all levels of education, and all political and religious beliefs. It is your responsibility to be respectful of those differences. That doesn't mean you have to like all of your fellow recruits and it doesn't mean you can resort to violence to "get them in line"; it means you have to find a way to interact like mature adults. Focus on the mission at hand and you will soon find that differences don't matter as much as teamwork.
- *Be the type of leader you would want to follow.* The Army wants its soldiers to be leaders, but being a leader doesn't mean that you are bossy or mean or that you look down on those below you. Think about the kind of leader you respect. What does he or she do that makes them a good leader? That is the type of per-

son you should strive to be when you are placed in a leadership role, both during basic training and after.

- *Take every opportunity to learn from those around you.* You will be amazing how much you will learn just from watching your fellow recruits, your drill sergeants, and the other personnel you encounter. Go into basic training believing that every person you meet will teach you something and be eager to accept those lessons.
- *Make friends.* You are training with the people who could one day stand beside you in combat. Get to know them, ask about their background and interests and reasons for enlisting, find out who they are. Having friends will make your time in basic training a shared experience rather than a solo survival expedition.
- *Take care of your body.* Injuries and illnesses will, at best, make training harder. At the worst, they could cause you to be set back in training or even put an end to training all together. Drink plenty of water. Keep your nails clipped, powder your feet, and tend to blisters. Wash your hands regularly, especially before eating or after going to the bathroom. If you hurt yourself or think you are sick, tell your drill sergeant immediately, no matter how fearsome he or she is. Drill sergeants are trained both to spot fakers and to see the signs of serious injury or illness, so he or she will know if you are well enough to continue training or if you need to visit a doctor.
- *Use "free time" to your advantage.* You won't get a lot of time to yourself, but you will get some and that time can help you recharge and regroup. Use free time to study, write letters to friends and family, and get to know your fellow recruits.
- *Develop a military bearing.* No matter what the situation, no matter how much you are being yelled at, no matter whose fault a problem is, you need to remain calm, collected, and mature. Don't whine, try to explain, or display emotions. If you act like you are calm and rational, then you will soon be calm and

rational, even when you are faced with combat stresses. Learn to let distractions — from biting flies to drill sergeants in your face to bombs going off around you — roll off your back.

- *Ask for help if you need it.* If you are injured, sick, or if you begin to have suicidal thoughts, you must ask for help immediately. Do not allow fear of your drill sergeant or of getting set back to keep you from getting the help you need. It is more important that you treat the problem up front, before it becomes a much bigger issue. Likewise, if you are having trouble understanding some aspect of training, ask your fellow trainees to help you study. They are likely to appreciate the chance to help you, especially since it means they'll be getting in valuable studying at the same time.

- *Remember that basic training is NOT what life in the military is like.* The goal of Army recruit training is to turn you from a civilian into a soldier. Your drill sergeants do this by breaking you down and then rebuilding you. After you graduate successfully from basic training, you will still have to work hard and remain professional, but you will not be faced with the same deprivations and strictures that you must live with during basic training.

- *Keep a positive attitude.* This can be hard, especially when you are feeling frustrated, tired, sore, discouraged, and/or homesick, but you have to stay positive. Think of each day as a new chance to try your hardest. Focus on the short term goal of getting through one day at a time and don't forget the long term goal or goals that led you to join the Army. Remember that thousands of men and women have gone through basic training successfully and you can too. At the end of each day, remind yourself of at least one good thing you accomplished that day and begin to look forward to the next day as another opportunity to learn. Each day is one day closer to you becoming a soldier!

Leaving for
Basic Training

During the weeks you've spent in the Delayed Entry Program, you've been working hard to get ready to leave for basic training. You should now be excited and eager and, most of all, ready to begin your new journey.

Final Preparations

As the time draws closer for you to leave for basic training, your recruiter will meet with you to go over your paperwork again. Make sure that everything is correct. Once you get to basic training, you will not be able to make changes. If something is not in your enlistment contract — whether it be a promotion, a job, or something else — then it doesn't exist. Read your contract carefully and make sure changes are made as soon as needed.

You will go back to the Military Entrance Processing Station (MEPS) to complete your paperwork, get reexamined by the doctors to make sure any medical issues have not arisen since your last visit, and to take the final Oath of Enlistment. Your recruiter will also make sure that nothing has happened to change your eligibility. During your time in the Delayed Entry Program you should have been keeping your recruiter apprised of any problems or changes that might affect your eligibility. It is better to address such issues now rather than wait until basic training. Once you take the final Oath of Enlistment and ship to basic training, you are bound by the Uniform Code of Military Justice and are subject to court-matial if you break military law.

After your recruiter has gone over your paperwork and after the doctors have looked you over again, then you will be discharged from the Delayed Entry Program. You then take the Oath of Enlistment for the second and final time. (If you are enlisting as a reservist, then you will not need to take the Oath again. You became a part of the military as soon as you took the Oath the first time.) As mentioned in Chapter 12: Visiting the Military Entrance Processing Station (MEPS), the Oath of Enlistment is a serious, solemn vow. You should not take it lightly. Read over it once more and make sure you are able to agree to it, freely and clearly.

> I, _____, do solemnly swear (or affirm) that I will support and defend the Constitution of the United States against all enemies, foreign and domestic; that I will bear true faith and allegiance to the same; and that I will obey the orders of the President of the United States and the orders of the officers appointed over me, according to regulations and the Uniform Code of Military Justice. So help me God.

Family members are welcome to attend your swearing of the Oath. After the ceremony is over, you should say good-bye to them, because you'll be leaving for basic training and they will not be able to go with you past this point.

Your travel to basic training will be arranged for you. Your recruiter will make sure that you know where you need to go and how you are getting there, whether you are traveling by bus or plane and whether or not you need to spend the night anywhere. All of your travel to basic training is paid for, as are any meals or hotel visits.

Packing for the Journey

Each branch of the military will give you a list of what to bring with you to basic training. The Army says you should bring with you ONLY:

- *Your wallet and any needed documents*: your Social Security Card, your driver's license or picture ID, your permanent resident alien/green card (if applicable), direct deposit form from your bank, and any other paperwork or documents your recruiter gives you or tells you to bring (such as your marriage certificate, your child/children's birth certificate(s), etc.)

- *Prescription medicines*: also bring a paper copy of the prescription from your doctor; this is assuming that the medicines have already been approved by the doctors at MEPS
- *Eyeglasses and contact lenses*: bring both even if you normally only wear contacts
- *Money*: at least ten dollars, but not more than fifty dollars in cash
- *Your recruiter's business card*
- *Wedding band* (if applicable)
- *Religious material* (if applicable): a medallion, a Bible, and/or a religious reference book
- *Small address book*: with your family and friends' contact information
- *Stationery and stamps*: if you go ahead and address and stamp the envelopes before you leave home, that will save you time later
- *Photos*: small ones are best; nothing pornographic
- *Padlock*: with two keys or a combination lock
- *Small duffel bag or gym bag*: bring a bag clearly marked with your name on the outside; this should hold the items you are required to bring with you
- *Towel and washcloth*
- *Toiletries*
  - All recruits should bring:
    - *Soap*: one bar of soap in a travel case
    - *Toothbrush and toothpaste*: toothbrush should be in a case
    - *Dental floss*
    - *Deodorant*
    - *Hairbrush or a 6 inch black comb*
    - *Shampoo*
    - *Nail clippers*
  - Male recruits should bring:

171

- *Razor, shaving cream, shaving kit*: only bring safety-type razors, not straight or electric
  - Female recruits can bring if desired:
    - *Hair care accessories*: elastics, bobby pins, etc. that match your hair color
    - *Razor, shaving cream or gel*: only bring safety-type razors, not electric
    - *Feminine hygiene items*: If it is your time of the month, you can bring supplies with you, but you do not need to bring enough for all of basic training, as you will have the opportunity to purchase more once you are issued supplies.
- *Clothing*
  - All recruits should bring:
    - *Civilian clothing*: one complete (tops, pants, underwear, socks) set of casual, comfortable clothes; make sure they are neat and clean, but that you are able to move in them
    - *Civilian shoes*: one pair; make sure they are comfortable; ideally, these should be the shoes you travel in
    - *Socks*: one pair of white, mid-calf, cotton athletic socks without colored bands or logos
    - *Shower shoes*: flip-flops/thong sandals; plain and simple is best
  - Male recruits should also bring:
    - *Underwear*: three pairs of white or neutral cotton briefs
  - Female recruits should also bring:
    - *Underwear*: eight pairs of white or neutral cotton underpants; no thongs
    - *Bras*: two white or neutral bras; these can be regular bras; you will purchase sports bras while you are receiving your supplies at the Reception Battalion
    - *Additional*: you may bring a white or neutral full slip and/or flesh-toned pantyhose, if you choose

You should not bring any weapons, playing cards, dice, pornography, food, gum, tobacco products, alcohol, illegal drugs, over-the-counter drugs (not even aspirin), jewelry (except for a wedding ring and/or a religious necklace), electronic devices (such as MP3 players or video game consoles), cameras, make-up, nail polish, large amounts of money, or any valuables.

Please note that your recruiter will give you the latest list of what you can and cannot bring with you to basic training. Follow that list exactly. It will save you a lot of hassle and insure that you are not singled out by the drill sergeants when you first get to training.

If you must bring a cellphone with you while you travel, it will be stored while you are in basic training. (BE SURE to turn it off as soon as you get on the bus to travel to the recruit training center.) You can bring a book or magazine with you if you need something to keep you occupied during your travels, but leave it at the airport or bus station for future passengers to enjoy. Since you don't need to bring much with you, leave large bags and purses at home. Bring a bag small enough to carry just your needed supplies.

You'll want to wear comfortable clothes for your journey, but make sure they look neat and professional. Khaki slacks with a polo or long sleeve shirt are good choices. Try to wear pants with pockets because you'll need a place to hold a pen and other items once you get to Reception. Roll down your sleeves, tuck in your shirt, and button your top collar button as soon as you get on the bus to the recruit training facility. You will be on your feet a lot, so wear shoes that support your feet. Closed-toe shoes with socks are best. Do not wear any earrings or nail polish. You do not want to stand out in any way when you arrive because that will guarantee that you will be harassed by instructors. Instead, aim to look bland and professional.

Men do not need to get a haircut before leaving for basic training (your head will be shaved soon enough!), but you should make sure your hair looks tidy. Women do not need to get their hair cut before training, even though they won't be getting their head shaved. But during training you'll need to keep your hair up and off your collar, so a shorter, easy to manage cut is a good idea. Before arriving at training, female recruits should put their hair into a bun or other neat hairstyle that keeps the hair off of their collar.

During Your Travels

Depending on where you are coming from, you may travel by van, bus, or airplane in order to get to basic training. Your recruiter will make sure you have all of the information and tickets you need to get to where you are going. If you live close enough where you do not have to fly, then you probably won't need a meal voucher. (Sometimes, though, kindly bus drivers will stop to allow new recruits to get one last fast food meal before they get to training.)

If you are coming from farther away, then you'll fly into the nearest large airport to your recruit training center and then take a bus or van from there. More than likely you'll get a meal voucher to spend at the airport. Be sure to throw away any leftover snacks or drinks before you get to basic training. You aren't allowed to bring them with you to the Reception Battalion.

You may be the only person from your town or region heading to boot camp, but you'll meet up with other recruits soon enough. These are the men and women you'll be training alongside, so be friendly and approachable. If there is a group of recruits traveling together, MEPS or your recruiter will appoint one recruit as a leader of the small group. It is the leader's job to make sure everyone gets to where they are supposed to be, when they are supposed to be there. The leader is also in charge of the group's official paperwork and must keep control of that paperwork at all times.

If you get separated from the group when traveling by air or if you run into any other problems, ask airport personnel to direct you to the nearest USO (United Service Organizations) office. There is usually a USO office in every airport and the personnel there can get you back on track. Otherwise, call your recruiter and explain the situation to him or her.

The United States Military Entrance Processing Command — the department that oversees all MEPS locations — has a video which explains recruit travel to basic training. It is particularly useful if you have never flown before, as it outlines all of the procedures for navigating through an airport. You can watch the video here: *http://www.mepcom. army.mil/travel-video.html.*

As mentioned before, you can bring a book or magazine to read while you are traveling and you should try to meet some of the other new recruits with whom you're traveling. But the most important thing you can do during your travels from home to recruit training is to rest. The days of Reception Week are long and sleepless and overwhelming. You will want to get as much rest beforehand as you can. All too soon your bus will be pulling up at the Reception Battalion and your civilian life will end as your new military life begins.

Reception Week

Though you will usually hear that Army basic training is ten weeks long, the main part of training is actually closer to nine. The first week is Reception Week and is not focused on training, but instead all about getting you processed into the Army. How long you stay there depends on when you arrive at basic training, but most recruits are there from three to seven days. While there you will fill out paperwork, get medical checkups, receive your gear, and finally, at the end, be added to a company and picked up by your drill sergeants.

Reception Week can in many ways be more stressful than the rest of basic training. You are confused, tired, homesick, and, most of all, afraid you have made a terrible mistake. To make it worse, there is a lot of "hurry up and wait," so you have time to worry about what you've gotten yourself into. But don't let yourself get down. Focus on how each part of the receiving and forming process brings you one step closer to being a soldier. Now is not the time to decide you do not want to go through basic training. You are here and you must continue. Failure to train will only land you in jail for disobeying orders.

Arriving at Basic Training

The Reception Battalion, which oversees Reception Week, must be highly organized in order to process the high number of recruits who arrive between Monday and Wednesday almost every week. Each of those days they get a call from the Army liaisons who are escorting recruits at the airport and other transportation stations with a head count, so that the Reception personnel know in advance how many recruits are arriving, when they will arrive, and their gender breakdown. When the bus carrying the new recruits passes through the gates of the basic training facility, the personnel at the gate call so that the drill sergeants at the Reception Battalion can be ready to get things started.

You will probably arrive at the recruit training depot at night, usually sometime between 8 P.M. and 2 A.M. When you arrive depends upon where you are traveling from and whether or not you have to wait for other recruits to join you. You might be on a bus filled with recruits or you could be in a passenger van with just a few other people. Either way, all new arrivals receive the same treatment. As soon as your bus or van pulls up to the Reception building, a drill sergeant will step on board and begin loudly informing you that you are to get off the vehicle in a rapid manner and line up in front of the doors of the building, men separated from women and active-duty enlistees separated from reserve enlistees. The drill sergeant will tell you to place your hands at your sides, with any bags at your feet. If you have not already done so, you will be instructed to roll down your sleeves, tuck in your shirt, and button your top collar button. Women will be told to pull their hair up off of their collar into a bun.

While you are standing at attention on the footprints, the drill sergeant will tell you that you are now an Army recruit, that you are subject to the Uniform Code of Military Justice (UCMJ) which means you may not be absent without leave (AWOL), and that you must at all times during your basic training be respectful through words, body gestures, and facial expressions. The drill sergeant may give you other instructions as well. Be sure to be close attention as those instructions will probably be important later in the reception process.

The First Night of Reception Week

Your first night at basic training will probably pass in a blur. You will do a lot of paperwork and there is also a lot of waiting. Your job during those hours is to listen, closely and carefully. There will be a lot of yelling, but if you pay attention and don't panic, then you will get through without too much trouble. If you have "free time," then study the Soldier's Blue Book that you will be issued almost immediately. It contains all of the information that you need to know to graduate, so the sooner you learn that information, the better off you'll be. The Soldier's Blue Book can be found online at *http://www.jackson.army.mil/sites/dss/docs/131*.

You will have a chance during Reception Week to call your family and them know that you have arrived, what your mailing address is, and that you will contact them closer to graduation to give them details on the graduation ceremony. You will not have much time to talk, only about five minutes, so use your time wisely. Ask them to be cheerful and supportive, so that you do not get upset.

In the beginning, you'll mostly be filling out paperwork. As soon as you enter the Reception Battalion, you will head to what looks like a classroom, complete with either tables or individual desks. You will be given paperwork to fill out and you will be told exactly how to fill it out. Do not fill in any information until you are told. Write only what you are told to write and do it as soon as you are told to do it. Over the course of the evening, you will fill out a lot of paperwork and some of it may seem repetitious, but it is all vital to getting you processed into the Army. The paperwork is important and will insure that you are properly processed, but — as with many things in basic training — it is also a way for the Army to get you used to following orders. One vital piece of information will be your battalion and company designations. You should memorize this information as soon as you are told it.

This first evening is also when you will turn in your personal effects, meaning the civilian clothes you arrived in, your cellphone, and other items which can be returned to you after training. You should not have brought much with you. (See Chapter 18 for a list of items to bring.) There will be a "Moment of Truth" where you can turn in any contraband, such as weapons, pornography, prescription drugs, etc. The Moment of Truth also allows you to confess to anything that you might not have told your recruiter about, such as a medical ailment like asthma or a minor criminal conviction. Ideally you will not have anything to report, since you will not have lied to your recruiter or omitted information. Lying during the Moment of Truth will not work as a way of getting out of basic training. The Army will be verifying anything you tell them and if they find that there is nothing preventing you from beginning training, then you *will* be beginning training. If your information is double-checked and it shows that you are ineligible for training, then you will begin processing to be sent back home.

After turning in your personal effects, you will change into your first uniform: Army t-shirts, sweatpants, and running shoes. You will be fed a boxed meal and shown to the Reception barracks. By this time it will be around 1 A.M., but you won't get much sleep. Instead a screaming drill sergeant will wake you up at 4 A.M. to continue the process of entering into Army recruit training.

Medical Testing and the Initial Strength Test

Much of the rest of Reception Week is taken up with medical testing. The doctors at basic training will put you through the same tests and evaluations that you underwent at MEPS. This is to ensure that any issues are caught before you begin training. It is important to remember that the doctors and nurses are not trying to disqualify you on purpose. They are only thinking of the greater good. What can be a simple problem for a civilian can be a major one for someone undergoing the rigors of military training. The medical personnel not only have to consider your safety and health, they have to consider how your physical issues will affect the units with which you will serve.

You will be drug tested again, so it should go without saying that you will not have been using any illegal drugs at any time before arriving at basic training. Female recruits will be tested for pregnancy and all recruits will be tested for sexually transmitted diseases. Additionally, you will visit the dentist who will evaluate your teeth and do any needed dental work. You will also visit an eye doctor who will check your eyes, verify your prescription (if you wear glasses or contacts), and issue you new, military-style glasses.

If major problems are found during your medical exams — problems which will prevent you from continuing training — you will be processed out of the Army. Unfortunately that is the end of your military career, unless the issue is a temporary one which will clear up in a matter of months. Once the processing is done, which can take anywhere from several days to a couple of weeks, you will be sent home.

The first few days of Reception Week is also when you will take your Initial Fitness Test (IFT). You must pass the IFT to continue on to basic training, but failing it will not get you sent home. Instead those recruits who fail the IFT or who are over the weight standards will be sent to the Fitness Training Company (FTC). FTC is aimed at getting out-of-shape and overweight recruits into good condition for training. (It also helps rehabilitate recruits who have been injured.) Recruits in FTC are given extra physical training to build them up and they cannot leave the FTC until they have passed the IFT. Time in the FTC does not count towards basic training, so it means extra weeks added onto your training. Here are the IFT goals you must meet in order to pass:

Event	IFT Minimum — Men
Run	1 mile run in 8 min. 30 sec.
Push-ups (in 2 min.)	13
Sit-ups (in 2 min.)	17

Event	IFT Minimum — Women
Run	1 mile run in 10 min. 30 sec
Push-ups (in 2 min.)	3
Sit-ups (in 2 min.)	17

The Rest of Reception

During the time when you are not undergoing medical or physical tests, you will begin receiving your gear. There is a lot of gear given to

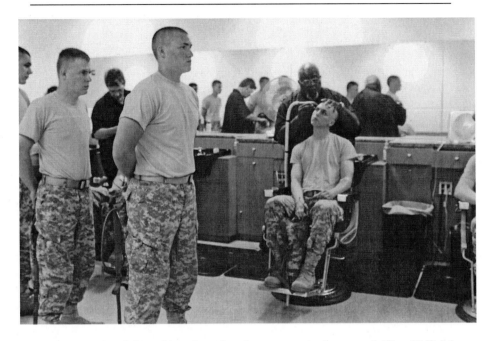

Getting your head shaved is a clear sign that you are no longer a civilian (Official U.S. Army photograph by Adrienne Anderson).

you during basic training and you are expected to account for it. Some of your gear is yours permanently and you are charged for it. The charges come directly out of your paycheck, so you don't need to have money with you. Other gear is only yours temporarily while you are training and you will have to return it. You will be issued everything from uniforms (including outerwear, underwear, socks, shoes, hats, and belts) to school supplies (a guidebook of essential information, notebooks, pens and pencils) to hygiene items (shampoo, laundry detergent, soap, toothpaste, towels, etc.) to military supplies (packs, canteens, rifles, rifle cleaning supplies, etc.), to miscellaneous items like stamps and padlocks.

The infamous haircuts are given during forming. All male recruits will have their heads shaved. This is done quickly by a team of civilian barbers and soon all the new recruits have the same hairstyle. Female recruits do not have their hair cut. They should arrive at the recruit training facility with their hair already neat and up off of their collar.

In addition to filling out paperwork, getting gear issued to you, and undergoing medical evaluations, during Reception Week you will learn how to make up your bed ("rack") in military fashion, learn how to address drill sergeants, and possibly even learn some basics of how to march. You will probably stand a guard during the night and you will start getting used to following directions quickly and correctly. Soon it will be time for you to meet the drill sergeants who will be in charge of you for the next nine weeks.

Once you have completed all of your paperwork, taken all of the required tests, and been issued your gear, you will finally join your company and be assigned to your permanent drill sergeants. This usually happens by Friday or Saturday of Reception Week. Now your drill sergeants will take some time to learn about their new company. They need to know who is left-handed, who is a reservist, what religions are represented, etc. They will make sure that you have all of your gear and that all your paperwork has been filled out and added to your file. They will get the company settled into the barracks and make sure that you know how to store your gear, make up your rack, and do what you're told to do.

During this time your drill sergeants will be trying to shock you out of any bad habits and make you realize that you are in the Army now. There is a lot of yelling and a lot of physical activity. You will feel like you cannot do anything right. That is the point. Your drill sergeants want you to feel like you are falling apart so that they can be the ones to put you back together as a soldier. As part of this, your drill sergeants will introduce you to "incentive training," physical activity used to punish you for not following orders, not doing something correctly, etc. You will probably also have a fire drill or some other simulated emergency, just to keep you off-balance.

For your part, you will begin to learn the basics of how to drill, how to wear your uniform, etc.—everything you need to know to understand basic training. You will attend your first religious services (if you so desire) on Sunday morning and your company will be ready to begin basic training the next day.

$\boxed{20}$

Life During
Basic Training

The schedule for what happens when during basic training only tells part of the story. You're probably still wondering about the basic, day-to-day aspects of boot camp life. No one can completely prepare you for what you'll experience during basic training, because every recruit's time at boot camp is different, but the general details remain the same for all enlistees.

Addressing Your Drill Sergeants

Every branch of the service has a different way that recruit training instructors should be addressed. In the Army, you should always address your drill sergeant as "Drill Sergeant [Name]" or "[Rank] [Name]." Do not use "sir" or "ma'am." While addressing your drill sergeant, you should look forward. Never stare them directly in the eyes. You have not yet earned that right.

Battle Buddies

The Army uses a system called Battle Buddies during basic training. The idea behind Battle Buddies is that you do everything with another soldier in training and that keeps the two of you from getting into trouble. Your drill sergeant will assign you your battle buddy. You do not get to pick and if there is someone that you show signs of not getting along with, it is likely he or she will be your battle buddy. Battle buddies are always the same gender, because you have to go everywhere with your battle buddy. If there is something you're good at, such as drill, then it is likely your battle buddy will be someone who is not good at drill. Your job, as their battle buddy, is to help him or her work on the things he or she is not as competent at doing. By the same token, he or she will help you build up your weaknesses. Since you cannot pick your battle buddy, you should just accept whomever you are assigned. Work hard to get along with him or her and your time in basic training will be easier.

Discipline and Punishment

Many people assume that drill sergeants can curse at, hit, bully, and abuse their recruits, but that is no longer the case. That does not mean, however, that drill sergeants have become gentle teddy bears. They are still allowed to "motivate" you, using a combination of yelling and physical fitness drills. Drill sergeants are known for their froggy-sounding voices. They get that way because they overwork their vocal cords screaming instructions at recruits. You will quickly learn how to understand what they are saying, because you want to be able to do what they want when they want it.

If you don't do what you are supposed to, then you'll most likely be disciplined using physical fitness drills. These drills are a series of exercises which are designed to get you in shape while also making you regret messing up. All exercises are carefully regulated and the drill sergeants have clear guidelines for using them.

Other acceptable punishments include removing your free time or assigning you to stand guard (waking up for an hour to keep watch while the other recruits sleep). You *will* experience some form of discipline during your time in recruit training, whether it is because you did something wrong or because your whole platoon messed up or because one person messed up and your drill instructor decided to make

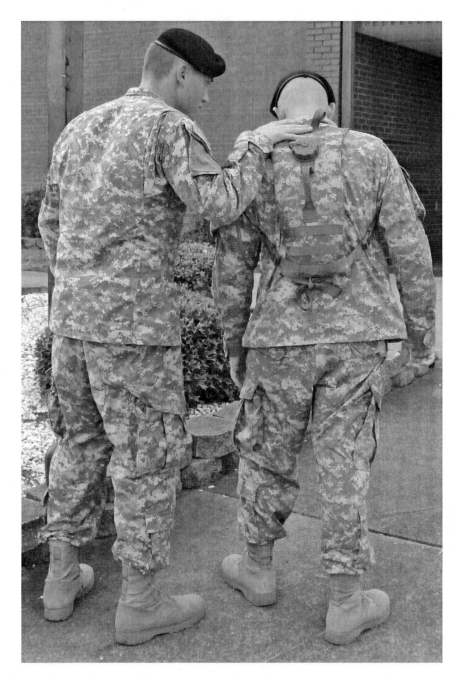

Battle buddies offer emotional as well as military support (Official U.S. Army photograph by Russell Sellers).

a point by punishing everyone. Whichever it is, know that it is coming and take it like a soldier.

Exodus

As of 2011, the Army shuts down all basic training for two weeks at the end of December. They are the only branch of the military that does this. Exodus allows all recruits and their instructors to go home and spend time with their families. If you are in training during December, you will be granted vacation, aka leave, at that time. However, it is not always a good idea to take that time off. If you do decide to go home during Exodus, be sure to follow some basic rules to keep yourself in good condition for when you resume training.

- *Practice moderation.* Do not overindulge in food or sugary drinks. Your system won't be used to them and you will likely make yourself sick.
- *Don't drink or smoke.* Even if you are of legal age, you have not been drinking alcohol or smoking while you were at training, so your system is not used to the effects of alcohol and cigarettes.
- *Don't use drugs.* You *will* be drug tested when you get back to basic training and if they find drugs in your system, you could be prosecuted for using them. Remember, you're an active-duty member of the military now and subject to the Uniform Code of Military Justice.
- *Practice safe sex.* Pregnancy or sexually transmitted diseases could also result in you getting kicked out of the Army.
- *Keep exercising.* Your body has gotten used to a high degree of daily activity. If you don't keep that up, then you will not be ready for the change when you head back to basic training.
- *Stick to a schedule.* Keep going to bed early and getting up early so that you don't lose the routine of basic training. Likewise, keep your belongings neat and organized, keep your bed made,

and follow the other military standards your drill sergeants have taught you.

- *Study*. You don't want to forget all of the things you have learned so far in basic training. Take all of your study materials with you and look over them every day while you are on break.
- *Stay focused emotionally*. Don't let yourself forget that you are going back to basic training. Stay determined to work hard when you get back. Ask your friends and family to be supportive and encouraging. They can do this by helping you look forward to returning to basic training, by exercising with you, by eating healthy meals with you, and by asking you to help them learn the things you have been learning.

You do not have to head home at Exodus. You can stay at basic training for whatever reason (too far to travel, no family, cannot afford the trip, etc.) Recruits who stay behind will be assigned duties to do, but they do not have classroom lessons during Exodus. If you do decide to take that leave, know that you will likely use up most of the vacation time you have been earning, as well as the vacation time you will earn while you are in your job training after basic training. That means that you will not be able to take vacation after you finish your job training.

Your best bet is to not be at basic training during the time that Exodus will occur. That may be out of your control, but if you want to avoid the issue, talk to your recruiter and see if your ship date can be adjusted so that you will not be affected by Exodus.

Food and Sleep

You'll be so active during basic training that food and sleep may be two of your major concerns. Recruits are guaranteed seven to eight full hours of sleep a night — with a few exceptions. When you are standing guard or keeping watch or when your company is doing night training exercises, your sleep time may be cut down to six hours. During your final field exercise, which is designed to see how you perform when overtired and stressed, you will get fewer hours of sleep per night.

During training you'll get three meals per day. These meals may be eaten in the dining facility, where you'll have a choice of hot foods and drinks, or you may be served portable meals eaten out in the field. Either way, you aren't given much time to eat — about 20 minutes — and you are not allowed to talk during the meal. Eat a balanced meal of proteins, vegetables, and carbohydrates, because you'll need the energy. Try to avoid sweets which will not stick with you between meals. During the summer months, you'll want to add extra salt to your food to replace the salt you lose through sweating. Some Army basic training locations have cut out sweets and sodas completely from the options available to recruits, in an effort to improve recruits' health.

Drill sergeants no longer force recruits to drink massive amounts

Staying hydrated by drinking plenty of water is one of the best ways to stay healthy during basic training (Official U.S. Army photograph by Crystal Lewis Brown, Fort Jackson Leader).

of water, since too much water is as bad for you as too little. Instead, you'll be issued a canteen and you'll have plenty of opportunities to refill it. In most of the restrooms you'll find a urine color chart. The chart shows you what color your urine should be if you are well-hydrated. (An example can be found here: *http://www.nmcphc.med.navy. mil/downloads/healthyliv/nutrition/urinekleurenkaart.pdf.*)

Free Time

Free time is time when you can study, read your mail, write letters, take care of personal issues, etc. During free time there will be a drill sergeant on duty and you can consult with him or her, but he or she will not be leading any instruction. You have the right to one hour of free time per day on Mondays through Saturdays and roughly four hours on Sunday mornings and holidays, but you won't always get that full amount. It can be curtailed as a discipline or because you are out in the field or other because of other issues. Overall, though, you will get free time every day and if your company has been especially good, your drill sergeant may be generous and give you two hours on a Saturday.

Graduation Requirements

In order to graduate from Army basic training, you must meet the following requirements:

- Pass the Army Physical Fitness Test (APFT) with a minimum of 50 points per event, 150 points total
- Qualify with your weapon, shooting a minimum of 23 out of 40, and with hand grenades
- Complete the obstacle and confidence courses, the gas chamber, the assigned foot marches, and the lifesaver course
- Pass the final Field Training Exercise

Housing

Except during field training exercises, recruits live in barracks. Barracks are a lot like dorms, except that you're sharing with a company of men or women instead of just one roommate! You'll sleep in bunk beds, arranged head-to-feet, meaning the feet of recruit in the top bunk are above the head of the recruit in the bottom bunk. The recruits in the bunk beds on either side are arranged in the opposite way. This helps prevent the spread of disease. One of the very first things you will learn is how to make a bed the military way — and how to do it quickly. During field training exercises, your accommodations will not be as grand. You could stay in huts or tents, depending on the training expectations.

Each recruit has his or her own storage space in the barracks. Drill sergeants will teach you how to arrange your belongings in a military manner. You are expected to maintain your storage lockers and your belongings at all times. Recruits are responsible for cleaning the barracks, the bathrooms, and the drill sergeants' areas. Your drill sergeants will look for dirt in the smallest of places, such as over the top of a window or a door. If they find it, then your whole company is likely to be disciplined.

Hygiene

You are given time each day to take care of personal hygiene, but not a lot of time. You'll learn the fast, Army way of taking a shower, shaving, going to the bathroom, brushing your teeth, and getting dressed each morning. And you'll do it all in front of everyone in your barracks. There are no private bathrooms in basic training; showers and sinks are communal. But you'll be hurrying too much to worry about being shy.

Female recruits will not usually have enough time to shave their legs. Drill sergeants don't give you enough time on purpose; nicks and cuts on freshly shaved legs can quickly become infected by grime picked up during training. But most female drill sergeants will give their recruits time to shave their legs before graduation or inspections.

There are portable bathrooms in the field and there are bathrooms in classroom areas, as well as in the barracks. Drill sergeants give recruits plenty of opportunities to use them, so you'll never need to worry about finding one when you need it. Female recruits may not get their periods during training because of the high level of activity and stress, but if they do, they simply carry supplies with them throughout the day. Supplies can be purchased at the Post Exchange as needed.

Male recruits have their heads shaved during Reception Week. They will visit the barbers each week for a trim. All of those haircuts are subtracted from their pay. Female recruits do not have their heads shaved, but they are expected to maintain neat and tidy hairstyles that keep the hair above the level of their collar. Women may have short hair or they may keep their hair in a bun. The important thing to remember is that any hairstyle you have must be able to be maintained neatly at all times, even when you are taking your helmet on and off. (Something to keep in mind — if you have your hair in a bun, you are slightly more anonymous since that is how many female soldiers wear their hair. That can be good for staying below the radar.)

The combination of lots of people, high stress, and the sweat and dirt of training means that you have to be extra careful to remain healthy during basic training. Remember to wash your hands after using the restroom and before eating in order to prevent the spread of disease. Do not share combs, brushes, personal grooming tools, canteens, etc., with your fellow recruits. Make sure you work hard to keep the barracks as clean as possible.

Leadership Roles and Recruit Jobs

The Army wants recruits to begin learning and practicing leading immediately, so there are a number of leadership positions that recruits can volunteer for or be assigned to. Whether you must volunteer or if you will simply be assigned to a leadership role is up to the whim of the drill sergeant. The Army offers three recruit leadership positions:

- Platoon Leader: this is the recruit who leads all other recruits in his or her unit, making sure the day-to-day operation of the company runs smoothly
- First Sergeant: assists the Platoon Leader
- Squad Leader(s): these recruit leaders work under the Platoon Leader, after receiving orders from the First Sergeant

You should know, though, that being a leader during basic training does put you in the spotlight and that means that you will be more closely scrutinized by drill sergeants. It is not uncommon for recruit leaders to be disciplined when one of the recruits they are in charge of messes up or if the drill sergeant does not think that the recruit leader has done a

Platoon Leaders should be models of Army core values for their fellow recruits (Official U.S. Army photograph by Crystal Lewis Brown, Fort Jackson Leader).

good job. Recruit leaders are often "fired" from their positions, but try not to take it personally. This is partially done to add to the stress of recruit training, but also to allow other recruits to have a chance to assume a leadership role.

The Army does have one other recruit job — the CQ (charge of quarters) Runner. The CQ Runner is the recruit who runs errands for the drill sergeant, going and getting information the drill sergeant needs or delivering messages.

Recycling or Getting Set Back

When you are recycled or set back in training, you are moved to another recruit training unit that is not as far along in training as the group you are currently assigned to. This can happen for a number of reasons. Sometimes it occurs for disciplinary reasons, because you have not followed instructions or have caused a serious violation. Other times recycling is done because you have not met the academic or physical standards that you need to in order to progress in training. If you fail a test or do not qualify in firing your weapon, then you can be set back to give you time to learn the skills you need to graduate. Recycling can also occur if you are injured or become seriously ill. For example, if you sprain your ankle during training, you will be given time to heal and then, because your training unit will have continued without you, you will be placed into a training unit that is at the same point in their training as you were when you were injured.

Religious Services

Army recruits come from a wide variety of religious backgrounds and the Army tries hard to make sure that all of their recruits are able to practice their faith. During the time when your drill sergeant is getting to know his or her company, you will be asked what religion you are. That will give them the information they need to plan for your religious needs. However, due to the demands of training, not all aspects of religious worship (such as Friday or Saturday services, special religious meals, or other religious requirements) may be able to be accommodated.

All religious services take place on Sunday mornings, regardless of the religion. Usually the base chapel will offer at the very least a Catholic service and a Protestant Christian service. Recruits who are Jewish, Buddhist, Muslim, Hindu, Latter Day Saints, Wiccan, and other religions will either attend services led by volunteers from the local community or will meet in groups led by the recruits themselves.

You are not required to attend religious services. If you do not currently practice any religion or if you are atheist, you can remain in the barracks during Sunday services. Or you are welcome to visit a different religious service each week to learn more about the faith. Some recruits attend services simply for the quiet and the break from training. On Sundays and during the week, Army chaplains are available to counsel recruits who are having trouble with some aspect of recruit training.

Safety, Injuries, and Illness

The personnel in charge of basic training are very careful to make it as safe as possible, even for a training regimen that involves live explosives! Drill sergeant training includes CPR, early detection of medical problems, suicide prevention, stress management, counseling techniques, and more. At every training location there are personnel to act as spotters and to assist recruits when needed. Medical personnel are on hand to treat injuries and illnesses and there are doctors and nurses stationed at the base hospital to treat more serious problems. Recruits are continually taught safety procedures, whether they are learning hand-to-hand combat or learning how to fire their weapons. Accidents still do happen, but the vast majority of the time they are due to a recruit's error, not to negligence on the part of training personnel. Be sure you pay close attention to all safety briefings and that you follow all instructions to the letter.

If you get injured or get sick, you will be allowed to visit a doctor. He or she will determine how serious your injury or illness is. For less severe injuries or illnesses, the doctor may prescribe a day or two of light duty or bed rest. Your drill sergeants will be informed of this decision and will know how to take care of you. Follow any instructions given to you so that you can get back into training shape as quickly as possible. Returning to full training too soon could lead to further damage to your body, which could delay your training.

Recruits who are too injured or too sick to continue training with their company are sent to a rehabilitation battalion. The rehabilitation battalion helps recruits heal from injuries and illness. Days in the rehabilitation battalion do not count towards training. If you miss too many days, you will probably be dropped back to join another company. Remember that this is for your safety and so that you have the opportunity to learn what you need to learn. Joining a new company midway through training is hard, but learning how to adapt to a new situation and how to become part of a new team is part of military life.

Uniforms and Supplies

When you check in during Reception Week you will get your initial issue of clothing, gear, toiletries, and supplies. The initial issue covers everything from underwear to razor blades to running shoes to stamps. You will also get a debit card which can be used at the Post Exchange to buy supplies and toiletries as you run out. During your time in basic training, you'll be issued even more gear and uniforms. Some of what you are issued, especially your uniform, is yours; you are paying for it and you'll need it for the future. Other gear, such as your M-16 rifle, is only yours during your time in basic training. It will be returned to supplies for the next recruit to use once you graduate.

Basic Training — Nine Weeks of Hard Work

Army basic training lasts nine weeks and is broken down into three phases: Red Phase, White Phase, and Blue Phase. Each of the Phases makes up roughly three weeks. Each week within those phases is designated by a different core value. The first Phase is Red Phase or "Patriot Phase" and its focus is total control — taking a civilian and making him or her completely responsible to his or her drill sergeant. After the first week of introduction, recruits focus on the core values of loyalty and duty. Phase two is White Phase or "Gunfighter Phase," where recruits learn how to handle weapons and focus on the core values of respect, selfless service, and honor. Basic training wraps up with Blue Phase or "Warrior Phase." During that time recruits put into practice all of the skills learned in basic training, including the core values of integrity and personal courage, finishing with graduation from training.

Nine weeks sounds like a lot of time — and it is — but there are ways to help yourself see the time passing. Set short, medium, and long-term goals. The short term is easiest: give each day your best effort. For a medium goal, focus on getting through the week, learning as much as you can. Your longest term goal is obviously to graduate successfully, but you should also focus on the end of the current Phase. As you move through the phases, you will begin to see how what you are learning all fits together.

Phase One: Red or Patriot Phase

After Reception you enter into Red Phase. While it may seem like you've already been in boot camp for a week — after all, you've been yelled at and ordered about since you got to Reception roughly six to eight days ago—this is the first day that counts towards graduation. From here on out you must complete the assignments, pass the tests, and learn the information presented to you over the next nine weeks or you will not graduate on time. Because Red Phase is the beginning of training, the drill sergeants are in total control. You will have no extra privileges until you and your unit show that you deserve them by successfully making it through to White Phase.

Red Phase is focused on teaching you the basics of learning to be a soldier—how to fight, how to wear a uniform, how the Army is organized, and how the Army expect you to behave. You will take classes in Army history, learning about the battles the soldiers have fought in and the people who have led and shaped the Army. You will participate in discussions of the first two Army Core Values: Loyalty and Duty. Each of these values is discussed in depth individually over the course of basic training, both by classroom teachers and by your drill instructors and the other five core values are added into the discussion as the weeks of training progress. There will be classroom courses on soldierization, land navigation, tactics, prisoners of war, sexual harassment, military justice, map-reading, race relations, and more.

You will also learn hands-on skills such as First Aid and bayonet techniques. You will run an obstacle course, a confidence course, and a teamwork development course, all designed to get you into shape, build your confidence in your ability to complete a difficult mission, and teach you and the others in your unit how to work together as a team. Recruits lean how to rappel, or go down the side of a building on a rope. Rappelling is another way to build confidence while learning military skills. Red Phase is where you begin the Army Physical Readiness Program. It is designed to get you into fighting shape. You will be doing the "toughening phase" of that program during recruit training. Toughening consists of exercises that make you jump, climb, lunge, bend, reach, and lift. Physical fitness exercises and drill and ceremony (learning to march in formation) are done almost every day of basic training.

The Army also begins training you to fight. Red Phase is when you get to fight with Pugil Sticks. Pugil Sticks look like oversized Q-Tips and they are designed to simulate combat with a bayonet, a blade that attaches to the front of a rifle. Recruits are paired off and try to use the sticks to knock each other out of the ring. It can look brutal, but it is a great way of working out aggression!

The second week is when you will most likely do the Nuclear, Biological, Chemical Training with Promask Confidence Exercise, aka the gas chamber. The gas chamber is designed to show you how your gas mask works so that you will have confidence in its abilities should you need to use it during combat. The chamber also teaches you not to panic while in a chemical or other hazardous material situation. After

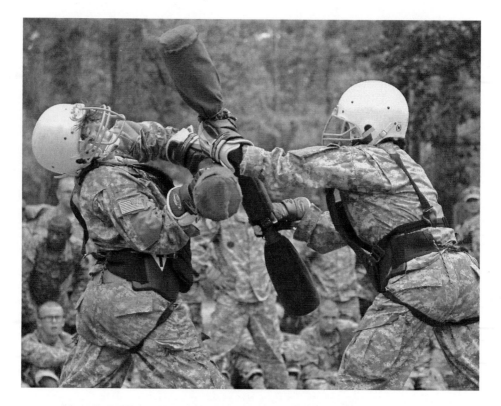

Pugil stick fighting is all about aggression (Official U.S. Army photograph by Air Force Staff Sgt. Stacy Pearsall).

instruction on using your mask, you will enter the chamber wearing your mask. Tear gas — a non-lethal gas used for riot control — will be released. You will have to take off your mask and repeat a series of information before you can leave the chamber. The gas will irritate your nose and throat, so you will cough and sneeze and your nose will run a *lot*. But remember not to panic — trust your equipment and trust your training — and know that the sensation will soon pass. You have to complete the gas chamber, so panicking will not help you. Recruits who don't complete will be sent back in as many times as needed until they do pass, so it is best to get it over with quickly the first time around!

At the end of Red Phase you will have your first field training exercise, where you go into the outdoors and put into practice the skills you have learned so far in classroom and practical lessons. During this time you and your fellow recruits must work as a team to complete your mission. In addition to this type of hands-on test, there will also

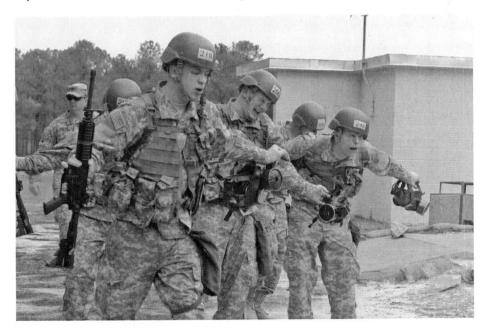

The gas chamber experience isn't pleasant, but it will give you confidence that your equipment works (Official U.S. Army photograph by Caroline Gotler).

be classroom tests on all of the information you have learned. You will need to pay close attention because the information you learn in Red Phase will be built upon in the White and Blue Phases.

Phase Two: White or Gunfighter Phase

White Phase's focus is on weapons training, but that doesn't mean that physical training and classroom learning are forgotten about. You will still be running, exercising, drilling, marching, visiting obstacle courses, and studying in the classroom. In addition to the classes on military topics, you will also be taking classes in core values, adding the values of Respect, Selfless Service, and Honor to the discussions of Loyalty and Duty. Assuming your unit has made it through Red Phase without major problems, your drill sergeants will slowly begin to give you a few more freedoms during White Phase.

During White Phase, you will have your Diagnostic Army Physical Fitness Test (APFT), which will show you how much your fitness has improved since you arrived at basic training and whether or not you are likely to pass the APFT at the end of basic training. You will have to get at least 150 points to graduate from basic training, but you will take the APFT again at the end of your advanced training and you will need to have 180 points then in order to graduate. If you can reach 180 points in basic training, then you will already be ahead of the game. Here are the requirements, broken down by age and gender:

Event	APFT 150 pts–Men (ages 17–21)	APFT 150 pts–Men (ages 22–26)	APFT 180 pts–Men (ages 17–21)	APFT 180 pts–Men (ages 22–26)
Run	2 mile run in 16 min. 36 sec.	2 mile run in 17 min. 30 sec.	2 mile run in 15 min. 54 sec.	2 mile run in 16 min. 36 sec.
Push-ups (in 2 min.)	35	31	42	40
Sit-ups (in 2 min.)	47	43	53	50

Event	APFT 150 pts — Women (ages 17–21)	APFT 150 pts — Women (ages 22–26)	APFT 180 pts — Women (ages 17–21)	APFT 180 pts — Women (ages 17–21)
Run	2 mile run in 19 min. 32 sec.	2 mile run in 20 min. 36 sec.	2 mile run in 18 min. 54 sec.	2 mile run in 19 min. 36 sec.
Push-ups (in 2 min.)	13	11	19	17
Sit-ups (in 2 min.)	47	43	53	50

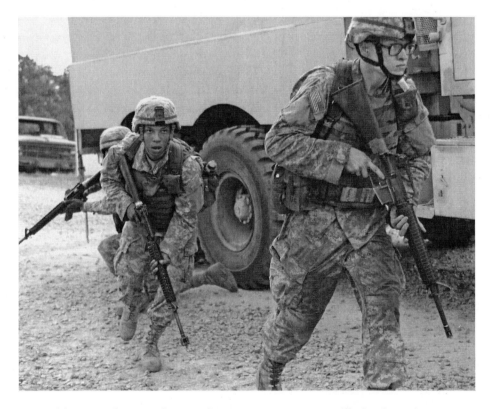

In addition to learning how to fire your weapon, you will also learn how to maneuver with it (Official U.S. Army photograph by Senior Airman Desiree N. Palacios, USAF).

The majority of White Phase is focused on teaching you how to properly fire your weapon. You will have already been learning the basics of your M16A2 rifle, even in Red Phase, but during White Phase you will learn both basic and advanced rifle marksmanship. An instructor will teach you the parts of your weapon, how to clean it, how to take it apart and reassemble it, how to aim, how to adjust your sights, how to fire, and how to take environmental conditions into account. You will learn how to fire alongside vehicles and while wearing body armor, both components of today's warfare styles, and you will learn how to shoot targets at a variety of distances. Even if you have never handled a weapon before, you will quickly learn the fundamentals. You won't immediately fire live ammunition. Instead you will first "dry-fire" your weapon, learning how to use it properly, before you move onto firing live ammunition. Finally you will have to qualify with your weapon in order to graduate, shooting at least 23 out of a possible 40.

There will be another field exercise during White Phase. Again, this is an opportunity for you to put to practice the skills you have learned so far in training. This field exercise, as well as the one from Red Phase, are meant to get you ready for the major field exercise at the end of Blue Phase, the one that you have to pass in order to graduate. Pass close attention and be sure to work on your teamwork.

Phase Three: Blue or Warrior Phase

During Blue Phase, the Army evaluates recruits to make sure they have learned what they need to learn in order to graduate. You will undergo inspections, march, take both written and hands-on tests, and have your final drill. There will still be classroom lessons, covering military information as well as core values. The values of Integrity and Personal Courage are added to the curriculum. Your drill sergeants will give you and your company more personal responsibility, assuming you have not made any major errors up to this point.

You will have to pass the Army Physical Fitness Test (APFT) with at least 150 points (50 from each event). It is best if you can pass with at least 180 (60 from each event), since that is what you will have to get to graduate from your advanced training. Here are the scores, broken down by age and gender:

Event	APFT 150 pts–Men (ages 17–21)	APFT 150 pts–Men (ages 22–26)	APFT 180 pts–Men (ages 17–21)	APFT 180 pts–Men (ages 22–26)
Run	2 mile run in 16 min. 36 sec.	2 mile run in 17 min. 30 sec.	2 mile run in 15 min. 54 sec.	2 mile run in 16 min. 36 sec.
Push-ups (in 2 min.)	35	31	42	40
Sit-ups (in 2 min.)	47	43	53	50

Event	APFT 150 pts — Women (ages 17–21)	APFT 150 pts — Women (ages 22–26)	APFT 180 pts — Women (ages 17–21)	APFT 180 pts — Women (ages 22–26)
Run	2 mile run in 19 min. 32 sec.	2 mile run in 20 min. 36 sec.	2 mile run in 18 min. 54 sec.	2 mile run in 19 min. 36 sec.
Push-ups (in 2 min.)	13	11	19	17
Sit-ups (in 2 min.)	47	43	53	50

Even though the APFT takes place towards the end of basic training, if you do not pass it, you will be sent to the Fitness Training Company (FTC) to get into better shape. That means that you will not graduate with the rest of your company.

Your classroom lessons will continue during Blue Phase, as you'll be learning what you need to know to complete the final field exercise. There will be classes on night infiltration, buddy team movements, military operations in urban terrain, field hygiene, and more. Many of these classes will be held outdoors, as there is both a classroom and a hands-on component to the training. You will learn about hand grenades — which are also a requirement for graduation — as well as anti-tank and other heavy weapons.

The culminating event for Army recruit training is a field training exercise. The exercise differs in name and length between the various training locations, but overall it is designed to test recruits on all aspects of what they have learned during basic training, from first aid to weapons firing and from teamwork to leadership. Recruits are stressed physically and mentally, working on low sleep and living in field conditions. These deprivations, along with the heavy gear, high amount of walking, and a soundtrack of combat noises are used to simulate combat stresses and see how the recruits handle them. During the field training exercise recruits will face problem solving exercises, man guard posts, learn how to deal with improvised explosive devices (IEDs), run maneu-

The final field training exercise is designed to simulate combat and allow you to put to the test the skills you learned in Basic Combat Training (Official U.S. Army photograph by Chris Rasmussen, Fort Jackson Leader).

vers, and more. There will be foot marches, night infiltration courses, and other events designed to prepare soldiers for combat.

Once the field training exercise is successfully completed, most locations will have some form of private ceremony acknowledging the recruits accomplishments. This varies from location to location and is not always a part of basic training. Recruits who are doing One Station Unit Training (OSUT) will continue on with training, though their drill sergeants will let them know that they have moved from Basic Combat Training to Advanced Individual Training. For graduates who are doing the traditional basic training, it is then time to get ready for final inspections and graduation.

$$\boxed{22}$$

Graduation and Beyond

Most of the last few days of Army Basic Combat Training revolve around getting ready for graduation. New soldiers turn in the gear that they aren't keeping and pick up the personal effects they dropped off at the Reception Battalion twelve weeks previously. Barracks are straightened and there is a rehearsal for Graduation.

Family Day and Graduation

Family Day is the day before Graduation, usually a Wednesday. First the Battalion Commander will meet with your family and friends to discuss basic training with them and answer any questions. Your guests will also get to meet your drill sergeants. Finally they will be reunited with you. You may be given liberty — time off— to spend with your friends and family on base, depending on your base's regulations and the decision of the chain of command. A few tips for family day liberty:

- *Your drill sergeants will give you clear instructions for how you are to behave. Follow these instructions to the letter.* Return on time at the end of the day. *DO NOT* mess up. Even if you are only one day away from graduation, you still have not graduated and you can be sent back to start training over.
- *Arrive early.* Remind your family that they will have to check in on base in order to be allowed to visit, so they need to allow time for that.
- *Obey all traffic laws.* Speed limits on base are often very slow,

usually 15–25 miles per hour. The Army takes these speed limits very seriously and your family will be pulled over if they violate them.

- *Don't overeat.* You'll be able to get food from wherever you like on base, but your stomach will not be used to soda and sweets and other junk food after so many weeks of doing without. You don't want to make yourself sick.
- *Take time to sit and catch up.* You'll want to show your family around base, but take some time to just sit quietly and talk. It will be the first time you've been able to see them in several months and you'll want to hear how they've been.
- *Include fellow soldiers whose families cannot come.* There will probably be at least one member of your company whose family cannot make it to graduation. Include him or her as a part of your family — after all, you are both soldiers now.

The Graduation ceremony is a proud moment. Recruits who have distinguished themselves in various ways will be recognized, as will any visiting dignitaries. There are a few tips to help make the day more enjoyable:

- *Don't make travel plans too early.* Your family should not make arrangements until you alert them to do so (usually during the early weeks of Blue Phase). There are a lot of things that can delay your training and they won't want to have to try to change plane tickets or hotel reservations if your graduation day changes. You will have arranged your own final travel details already, so you will have a way to get to your next phase of training.
- *Dress for the weather.* Depending on where you are training, the weather could be very hot or could be very cold. Tell your family to bring weather appropriate clothes, especially if they are not used to being in the part of the country where your training facility is located. If it is raining or snowing, Graduation will be moved indoors.
- *Dress appropriately.* Families can either dress up for the ceremony,

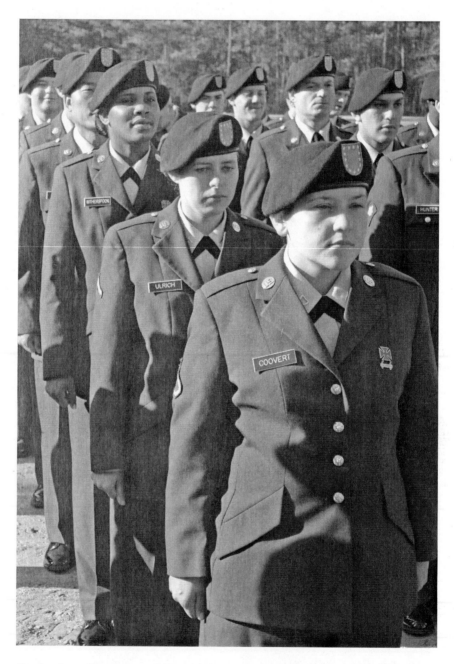

Graduation allows new soldiers to show their skills and discipline off to their loved ones (Official U.S. Army photograph by Chris Rasmussen, Fort Jackson Leader).

just as they would for a high school or college graduation, or they may choose to wear shirts with your company, platoon, or battalion information on it. Either is appropriate and acceptable.

- *Bring something to occupy small children.* Graduation is not long, but the ceremony can be too dry for small children. Bring books or small, quiet toys to keep them occupied.

If your family cannot come to graduation because of financial reasons, there are often groups who might be able to help. Check with your house of worship or local Army reserve unit to see if they might have a program to assist families in attending graduation.

After Graduation

And now you are a soldier. Congratulations! But your journey has just begun. You still have more training to go through before you'll actually begin doing the job you signed on to do. After Graduation, which is usually on a Thursday, you will have a little bit of time to spend with your family. But you will have to be back on base first thing on Friday morning to leave for Advanced Individual Training (AIT). You will travel immediately to AIT and begin studying the Monday following your arrival. You will not receive any leave time (vacation) until after your AIT course is over. Training at AIT schools can last from a month to over a year, depending upon what your Military Occupational Specialty is. From there you'll be sent to your first permanent duty station and begin your career as a soldier.

Glossary of Military Terms

Active Duty—those military personnel who serve full time

AFQT: The Armed Forces Qualifying Test—a part of the ASVAB; made up of four tests that measure your knowledge of math and language skills; the AFQT used to determine your eligibility for military enlistment

Air Force—the branch of the military responsible for air warfare

Allowances—moneys which help military personnel pay for housing, food, uniforms, etc.

Army—the branch of the military responsible for land warfare

ASVAB: the Armed Services Vocational Aptitude Battery—a series of tests taken to determine your skills and knowledge; used for job placement in the military

Barracks—dormitory style housing on military bases

Basic Training or Recruit Training (also called Boot Camp)—the initial training for new enlisted military personnel; lasts between seven and thirteen weeks depending upon the branch of the service

CAST: Computer Adaptive Screening Test or *EST: Enlistment Screening Test*—a mini–ASVAB test taken in a recruiter's office which shows what a potential enlistee's AFQT score will probably be; used to help potential enlistees know if their scores will qualify them for enlistment

CAT: Computer Adaptive Test—name of the ASVAB test when taken on computer

Chaplain—the military term for a religious leader, preacher, minister, rabbi, imam, etc.

Civilians—those persons not serving in the military

Coast Guard—the branch of the military responsible for law enforcement on the waters (lakes, rivers, etc.) in and around the United States

Commissary—a grocery store on a military base

Conscientious Objector—someone who refuses to fight or participate in any war because of religious, personal, moral, or ethical beliefs

DEP: Delayed Entry Program—the period of time between finalizing the enlistment process and leaving for basic training; length varies from a few weeks to 365 days

Dependents—any people that a military person has to take care of: a spouse, any children or stepchildren (living in the home) who are under 18 and unmarried, and any other family members who rely on a military member for more than half of their support

DoD: Department of Defense—the government agency that oversees four branches of the military—Air Force, Army, Navy, Marines; the Coast Guard is under the Department of Homeland Security

Don't Ask, Don't Tell—a policy put in place in 1993 which allowed homosexuals to serve in the military, but only if they did not tell anyone their sexual orientation or participate in homosexual activities (i.e., sex or gay marriage); overturned in December 2010; fully repealed in September 2011

Drill Sergeant—the Army term for the person in charge of recruits during recruit training

Enlisted—those military personnel who are responsible for the daily operations of the military under the command of officers; ranks range from E-1 to E-9

Enlistment Process—the steps taken to join the military as an enlisted person

Exchange—a department or general goods store on a military base

Incentive Pay—special pay which some military personnel earn because of the job they do or the risks to which they are exposed

IRR: Individual Ready Reserve—former military personnel who do not drill or receive pay, but who can still be called up to active duty; the last years of an enlistment are spent in the IRR

Marine Corps— the branch of the military responsible for amphibious (sea-to-land) warfare

MEPS: Military Entrance Processing Station— a Department of Defense facility that is in charge of physical and mental exams of potential enlistees, as well as administering the Oath of Enlistment and shipping new recruits off to basic training

MET: Mobile Examining Team— a facility that exists solely to administer the ASVAB test to potential enlistees

MOS: Military Occupational Specialty— the job field you will be assigned and trained in

MRE: Meal-Ready-to-Eat— portable, long-lasting, prepackaged meal eaten during field maneuvers and combat

National Guard— the reserve military programs that are managed by individual states, rather than by the Federal Government; there are two: Army National Guard and Air National Guard (Air Force)

Navy— the branch of the military responsible for warfare on the sea

NCOs: Non-commissioned officers— the upper enlisted ranks; NCOs act as leaders and managers; generally the ranks of E-4 to E-9, with E-4 to E-6 called junior NCOs and E-7 to E-9 called senior NCOs

Oath of Enlistment— the official swearing-in pledge that all new recruits take just before leaving for basic training

Officers— the command personnel of the military branches; ranks range from O-1 to O-9

PAP: Paper and Pencil— name of the ASVAB test taken on paper

Pay grade— the level of pay a particular military member is eligible for each month

Post-9/11 GI Bill— the most commonly used education programs for all branches of the military; it provides money for tuition and other expenses

Rank— the position you hold within the military; can be enlisted, warrant officer, or officer

Recruiter— the military man or woman who is responsible for giving out information about joining the military, finding candidates for enlistment, checking their qualifications, guiding them through the enlistment process, and offering tips on how to prepare for recruit training

Reserves— those military personnel who serve part-time, training one weekend a month and two weeks a year; they can be called up to active duty when needed

Stop Loss— a program which allows the military, during times of conflict, to prevent personnel from leaving the military on their normal separation date for up to one year; used during times of war to keep needed personnel on active duty

Technical Subtests— a part of the ASVAB; made up of five tests that measure your knowledge of and aptitude (natural talent) for technical skills; the technical subtests are used to determine which jobs you are eligible for

Tricare— the military's health care plan

UCMJ: Uniform Code of Military Justice— the official military laws of the United States, parts of which cover the criminal prosecution of military personnel

USO: United Services Organizations, Inc.— a private, nonprofit group that support military personnel by providing morale, welfare, and recreational services

Waiver— official approval that allows someone to enlist in the military despite not meeting a particular qualification or qualifications

Warrant Officers— a specialty rank that falls in-between enlisted personnel and officers; the Air Force is the only branch that does not have Warrant Officers

For More Information

Further Information about the Army and the United States Military

BOOKS

Axelrod, Alan. *Encyclopedia of the U.S. Army*. New York: Checkmark, 2006.

A Day in the Life of the United States Armed Forces. New York: Epicom Media, 2003.

Department of the Army. *The Soldier's Guide: The Complete Guide to U.S. Army Traditions, Training, Duties, and Responsibilities*. New York: Skyhorse Publishing, 2007.

Dolan, Edward F. *Careers in the U.S. Army*. Military Service. New York: Marshall Cavendish/Benchmark, 2010.

Rush, CSM Robert S., USA (Ret.), reviser. *Enlisted Soldier's Guide*. 7th Edition. Mechanicsburg, PA: Stackpole Books, 2006.

Schading, Barbara. *A Civilian's Guide to the U.S. Military: A Comprehensive Reference to the Customs, Language, and Structure of the Armed Forces*. Cincinnati, OH: Writer's Digest, 2007.

VIDEOS

Army Media Player: *http://www.army.mil/media/amp/*.

Inside Today's Military: *http://www.todaysmilitary.com/inside*.

WEBSITES

About.com's U.S. Military site: *http://usmilitary.about.com*.

Department of Defense's Official Site: *http://www.defense.gov*.

Military.com: *http://www.military.com*. [NOTE: To access some information on Military.com, you will have to register and your information will be shared with recruiters.]

Military Woman: *http://www.militarywoman.org*.

Today's Military: *http://www.todaysmilitary.com.*
United States Army's Official Site: *http://www.army.mil.*

Military Career Planning

BOOKS

Careers in Focus: Armed Forces. New York: Ferguson, 2008.
Goldberg, Jan. *Careers for Patriotic Types and Others Who Want to Serve Their Country.* Careers for You. 2nd edition. New York: McGraw-Hill, 2006.
Henderson, C.J., and Jack Dolphin. *Career Opportunities in the Armed Forces.* 2nd edition. Revised by Pamela Fehl. New York: Ferguson, 2007.
150 Best Jobs Through Military Training. Indianapolis, IN: JIST, 2008.
Sterngass, Jon. *Armed Forces.* Great Careers with a High School Diploma. New York: Ferguson, 2008.

WEBSITES

ASVAB Career Exploration Program: *http://www.asvabprogram.com.*
Military Career Information: *http://usmilitary.about.com/od/theorderlyroom/u/career_info.htm.*
Military Careers: *http://www.todaysmilitary.com/careers.*
My Future: *http://www.myfuture.com.* [This is a Department of Defense website that brings together information about careers, colleges, and military service provided by the Departments of Commerce, Defense, Education and Labor.]

Military Benefits

BOOK

Michel, Christopher P., and Terry Howell. *The Military Advantage: The Military.com Guide to Military and Veterans Benefits.* 2010 edition. Annapolis, MD: Naval Institute Press, 2010.

WEBSITES

Defense Finance and Accounting Service — Military Pay: *http://www.dfas.mil/militarypay.html.*
Department of Veterans Affairs' GI Bill Site: *http://www.gibill.va.gov.*
Department of Veterans Affairs' Jack-of-All-Trades page: *http://www.gibill.*

va.gov/bill-of-all-trades/index.html [Gives information on non-college programs that are supported by the GI Bill]

Department of Veterans Affairs' WEAMS Institution Search: *http://inquiry.vba.va.gov/weamspub/buildSearchInstitutionCriteria.do* [Allows you to search for continuing education programs which will be covered by the GI Bill.]

Military Benefits: *http://www.military.com/Benefits.*

Military Benefits: *http://www.myfuture.com/military/articles-advice/military-benefits.*

Military Pay and Benefits: *http://usmilitary.about.com/od/militarypay/u/pay_and_benefits.htm.*

So Much More Than Just a Paycheck: *http://www.todaysmilitary.com/benefits.*

Understanding the Post–9/11 GI Bill: *http://images.military.com/media/education/pdf/post911_gibill.pdf*

Enlistment Information

BOOK

Ostrow, Scott. *Guide to Joining the Military.* 2nd edition. Lawrenceville, NJ: ARCO, 2003.

VIDEO

A Day at the MEPS: *http://www.mepcom.army.mil/video.html*

WEBSITES

Joining the Military: *http://usmilitary.about.com/od/joiningthemilitary/u/joining_up.htm.*

10 Steps to Joining the Military: *http://www.military.com/Recruiting.*

U.S. Army's Official Recruiting Site: *http://www.goarmy.com.*

Army Recruiting Command

Use this contact information to report inappropriate behavior on the part of a recruiter.

E-mail: Secretary of the General Staff: sgs-usarec@usaac.army.mil

Telephone: (877) 437–6572

Mail: United States Army Recruiting Command, 1307 3rd Avenue, Fort Knox, KY 40121

ASVAB: Information and Study Guides

BOOKS

Ostrow, Scott A. *Master the ASVAB.* 21st ed. Lawrenceville, NJ: Thomson/ Arco, 2008. [Includes information on military careers.]

Powers, Rod. *ASVAB AFQT for Dummies.* Hoboken, NJ: Wiley, 2010.

Powers, Rod, and Jennifer Lawler. *ASVAB for Dummies.* 2nd ed. Hoboken, NJ: Wiley, 2007. [Includes information on which subtests correspond to which military job.]

Stradley, Laura, and Robin Kavanagh. *The Complete Idiot's Guide to the ASVAB: Time-Tested Techniques for Acing the ASVAB!* New York: Alpha, 2010.

WEBSITES

ASVAB Career Exploration Program: *http://www.asvabprogram.com.*

ASVAB's Official Site: *http://www.official-asvab.com.*

March2Success: *https://www.march2success.com.* [A test-prep site developed by the U.S. Army.]

Life During Army Recruit Training

BOOKS

Herbert, Don. *63 Days and a Wake-Up: Your Survival Guide to United States Army Basic Combat Training.* New York: iUniverse, 2007.

Powers, Rod. *Basic Training for Dummies.* Hoboken, NJ: Wiley, 2011.

Volkin, Sergeant Michael. *The Ultimate Basic Training Guidebook: Tips, Tricks, and Tactics for Surviving Boot Camp.* 4th edition. New York: Savas Beatie, 2009.

Volkin, Sergeant Michael. *The Ultimate Basic Training Workbook: What You Must Know to Survive and Thrive.* New York: Savas Beatie, 2007.

VIDEOS

Basic Training—The Ten-Week Journey from Civilian to Soldier: *http://www.goarmy.com/soldier-life/becoming-a-soldier/basic-combat-training.html.*

Recruit Travel Video: *http://www.mepcom.army.mil/travel-video.html.* [Tells new recruits the procedures that should be followed while traveling to basic training.]

Websites

Fort Benning: *https://www.benning.army.mil/basictraining.*
Fort Jackson: *http://www.jackson.army.mil/sites/bct.*
Fort Leonard Wood: *http://www.wood.army.mil/wood_cms/252.shtml.*
Fort Sill: *http://sill-www.army.mil/434.*
The Soldier's Blue Book: The Guide for Initial Entry Training Solidiers: available at http:www.jackson.army.mil/sites/dss/docs/131.

Books for Younger Readers

Benson, Michael. *The U.S. Army.* U.S. Armed Forces. MN, Minn.: Lerner, 2005.
Demarest, Chris L. *Alpha Bravo Charlie: The Military Alphabet.* New York: Margaret K. McElderry Books, 2005.
Goldish, Meish. *Army: Civilian to Soldier.* Becoming a Soldier. New York: Bearport, 2011.
Hamilton, John. *The Army.* Defending the Nation. Edina, MN: Abdo, 2007.

Resources

Allison, Aimee, and David Solnit. *Army of None: Strategies to Counter Military Recruitment, End War, and Build a Better World.* New York: Seven Stories, 2007.

American Women and the United States Armed Forces: A Guide to the Records of Military Agencies in the National Archives Relating to American Women. Compiled by Charlotte Palmer Seeley. Revised by Virginia C. Purdy and Robert Gruber. Washington, DC: National Archives and Records Administration, 1992.

Ashabranner, Brent. *A Date with Destiny: The Women in Military Service for America Memorial.* Photographs by Jennifer Ashabranner. Great American Memorials series. Brookfield, CT: Twenty-first Century Books, 2000.

Axelrod, Alan. *Encyclopedia of the U.S. Army.* New York: Checkmark, 2006.

Baker, Anni. *Life in the U.S. Armed Forces: (Not) Just Another Job.* Westport, CT: Praeger Security International, 2008.

Benson, Michael. *The U.S. Army.* U.S. Armed Forces. Minneapolis, MN: Lerner, 2005.

Bradford, James C., ed. *International Encyclopedia of Military History.* New York: Routledge, 2006.

Buckley, Gail. *American Patriots: The Story of Blacks in the Military from the Revolution to Desert Storm.* Adapted by Tonya Bolden. New York: Crown, 2003.

Bumiller, Elisabeth. "Letting Women Reach Women in the Afghan War." *The New York Times,* March 6, 2010. http://www.nytimes.com/2010/03/07/world/asia/07women.html.

Burns, Robert. "Ask and Tell: 18-year Ban of Gays in Military Is Lifted." *Charlotte Observer,* September 21, 2011, sec. A.

_____. "Military Is 'Adequately Prepared' to End Ban on Gays, Says Pentagon." *Charlotte Observer,* September 20, 2011, sec. A.

Careers in Focus: Armed Forces. New York: Ferguson, 2008.

Chambers, John Whiteclay II, ed. *The Oxford Companion to American Military History.* New York: Oxford University Press, 1999.

Collins, Robert F. *Basic Training: What to Expect and How to Prepare.* Military Opportunity. New York: Rosen, 1988.

Cooper, Jason. *U. S. Army.* Fighting Forces. Vero Beach, FL: Rourke, 2004.

Defense Finance and Accounting Service. "Military Pay Tables—1949 to 2011." http://www.dfas.mil/militarymembers/payentitlements/military paytables.html.

Department of Defense. *Personnel & Procurement Reports and Data Files.* DoD Personnel & Procurement Statistics. http://siadapp.dmdc.osd.mil.

Dillon, C. Hall. "The Military Offers Valuable Training for Civilian Careers." In *Choosing a Career,* edited by Linda Aksomitis. Issues That Concern You. Detroit: Gale, 2008.

Dolan, Edward F. *Careers in the U.S. Army.* Military Service. New York: Marshall Cavendish/Benchmark, 2010.

Dorr, Robert F. *Alpha Bravo Delta Guide to the U.S. Army.* Walter J. Boyne, series editor. Indianapolis, IN: Alpha, 2003.

Doubler, Michael D. *The National Guard and Reserve: A Reference Handbook.* Contemporary Military, Strategic, and Security Issues. Westport, CT: Praeger Security International, 2008.

Dribben, Melissa. "Sexual Assault a Silent Battle for Servicewomen." *Charlotte Observer,* September 18, 2011, sec. A.

Gavin, Lettie. *American Women in World War I: They Also Served.* Niwot: University Press of Colorado, 1997.

Gay, Kathlyn. *The Military and Teens: The Ultimate Teen Guide.* It Happened to Me, No. 21. Lanham, MD: Scarecrow, 2008.

Gibbs, Nancy. "Sexual Assaults on Female Soldiers: Don't Ask, Don't Tell." *Time,* March 8, 2010. http://www.time.com/time/magazine/article/0, 9171,1968110,00.html.

Goldberg, Jan. *Careers for Patriotic Types and Others Who Want to Serve Their Country.* Careers for You. 2nd ed. New York: McGraw-Hill, 2006.

Goldstein, Joshua S. *War and Gender: How Gender Shapes the War System and Vice Versa.* Cambridge: Cambridge University Press, 2001.

Hamilton, John. *The Army.* Defending the Nation. Edina, MN: Abdo, 2007.

Harris, Bill. *The Complete Idiot's Guide to Careers in the Military.* Indianapolis, IN: Alpha, 2002.

Hearn, Chester G. *Army: An Illustrated History—The U.S. Army from 1775 to the 21st Century.* Minneapolis, MN: Zenith, 2006.

Henderson, C.J., and Jack Dolphin. *Career Opportunities in the Armed Forces.* 2nd ed. Revised by Pamela Fehl. New York: Ferguson, 2007.

Herbert, Don. *63 Days and a Wake-Up: Your Survival Guide to United States Army Basic Combat Training.* New York: iUniverse, 2007.

Kilpatrick, Kelly. "Things to Consider Before Joining the US Military." *US Military.* About.com. http://usmilitary.about.com/od/joiningthemilitary/a/consider.htm.

Leff, Lisa. "Active-Duty Gays: Coming Out Has Been Nonevent." *Army Times,* October 16, 2011. http://www.armytimes.com/news/2011/10/ap-military-dont-ask-dont-tell-gays-coming-out-nonevent-101611.

Michel, Christopher P., and Terry Howell. *The Military Advantage: The Military.com Guide to Military and Veterans Benefits.* 2010 ed. Annapolis, MD: Naval Institute Press, 2010.

Military.com. "Learn to Use Your GI Bill Benefits." *Education.* http://www.military.com/education/content/gi-bill/learn-to-use-your-gi-bill.html.

_____. "Military Benefits." *Benefits.* http://www.military.com/Benefits.

Monahan, Evelyn M., and Rosemary Neidel-Greenlee. *A Few Good Women: America's Military Women from World War I to the Wars in Iraq and Afghanistan.* New York: Knopf, 2010.

Nathan, Amy. *Count on Us: American Women in the Military.* Washington, DC: National Geographic Society, 2004.

Ordoñez, Franco. "Military Gets Ready for a New Era." *Charlotte Observer,* August 28, 2011, sec. A.

Ostrow, Scott A. *Guide to Joining the Military.* 2nd ed. Lawrenceville, NJ: Thomson/Arco, 2004.

_____. *Master the ASVAB.* 21st ed. Lawrenceville, NJ: Thomson/Arco, 2008.

Paradis, Adrian A. *Opportunities in Military Careers.* Rev. ed. New York: McGraw-Hill, 2006.

Parker, Ashley. "Lawsuit Says Military Is Rife with Sexual Abuse." The *New York Times,* February 15, 2011. http://www.nytimes.com/2011/02/16/us/16military.html.

Philpott, Tom. "Gay Benefits Rules Drafted." *Headlines.* Military.com, December 2, 2010. http://www.military.com/features/0,15240,223455,00.html.

Porterfield, Jason. *Frequently Asked Questions About College and Career Training.* Teen Life. New York: Rosen, 2009.

Powers, Rod. *US Military.* About.com. http://usmilitary.about.com.

_____, and Jennifer Lawler. *ASVAB for Dummies.* 2nd ed. Hoboken, NJ: Wiley, 2007.

Rosen, James. "First Lady to Visit Army Base in S.C." *Charlotte Observer,* January 24, 2011, sec. A.

Rush, CSM Robert S., USA (Ret.), reviser. *Enlisted Soldier's Guide.* 7th Edition. Mechanicsburg, PA: Stackpole Books, 2006.

Schading, Barbara. *A Civilian's Guide to the U.S. Military: A Comprehensive Reference to the Customs, Language, and Structure of the Armed Forces.* Cincinnati, OH: Writer's Digest, 2007.

Stalsburg, Brittany L. "After Repeal: LGBT Service Members and Veterans: The Facts." *Publications.* Service Women's Action Network, 2011. http://servicewomen.org/wp-content/uploads/2011/10/LGBT-Fact-Sheet-091411.pdf.

_____. "Rape, Sexual Assault and Sexual Harassment in the Military: The Quick Facts." *Publications.* Service Women's Action Network, 2011. http://servicewomen.org/wp-content/uploads/2011/09/R-SASH-Quick-Facts-081811.pdf.

Stewart, Gail B. *Fighting for Freedom: Blacks in the American Military.* Lucent Library of Black History. Detroit, MI: Thompson Gale, 2006.

Stradley, Laura, and Robin Kavanagh. *The Complete Idiot's Guide to the ASVAB: Time-Tested Techniques for Acing the ASVAB!* New York: Alpha, 2010.

Tate, Curtis. "Pentagon Lets Chaplains Perform Gay Weddings." The *Charlotte Observer,* October 1, 2011, sec. A.

Thompson, Peter. *The Real Insider's Guide to Military Basic Training: A Recruit's Guide of Important Secrets and Hints to Successfully Complete Boot Camp.* Rev. ed. Universal Publishers/uPUBLISH.com, 2002.

Understanding the Post-9/11 GI Bill. Military Advantage, 2009. http://images.military.com/media/education/pdf/post-911-gi-bill.pdf.

United States Army. *Official Site.* http://www.army.mil.

United States Census Bureau. *Statistical Abstract.* http://www.census.gov/compendia/statab.

United States Department of Veterans Affairs. *GI Bill Web Site.* http://www.gibill.va.gov/

United States Federal Government. "U.S. Code TITLE 10 > Subtitle C > PART I > CHAPTER 31 > § 502. Enlistment Oath: Who May Administer." *Legal Information Institute.* Cornell University Law School. http://www.law.cornell.edu/uscode/html/uscode10/usc_sec_10_00000502----000-.html.

_____. "U.S. Code TITLE 10 > Subtitle C > PART I > CHAPTER 507 > § 5063. United States Marine Corps: Composition; Functions." *Legal*

Information Institute. Cornell University Law School. http://www.law.cornell.edu/uscode/10/5063.html.

United States Military Entrance Processing Command. *Enlistment Processing*. http://www.mepcom.army.mil/enlistment.html

_____. *USMEPCOM Videos*. http://www.mepcom.army.mil/MEPCOM_videos.html.

Vaughn, Kirby Lee. *The Enlistment Planning Guide: How to Make the Most of Your Military Service*. Santa Barbara, CA: Essayons Publishing, 1995.

Volkin, Sergeant Michael. *The Ultimate Basic Training Guidebook: Tips, Tricks, and Tactics for Surviving Boot Camp*. 4th ed. New York: Savas Beatie, 2009.

Watson, Cynthia A. *U.S. Military Service: A Reference Handbook*. Contemporary World Issues. Santa Barbara, CA: ABC-CLIO, 2007.

Watson, Julie. "For Gay Troops, Changes Precede End of DADT." *Marine Corps Times*, September 18, 2011. http://www.marinecorpstimes.com/news/2011/09/ap-for-gay-troops-changes-precede-end-of-dadt-091811.

Weill-Greenberg, Elizabeth, ed. *10 Excellent Reasons Not to Join the Military*. New York: The New Press, 2006.

Women in Military Service for America Memorial Foundation, Inc. "Statistics on Women in the Military." *For the Press*. http://www.womensmemorial.org/PDFs/StatsonWIM.pdf.

Women's Army Corps Veterans' Association. *Official Site*. http://www.armywomen.org.

Youssef, Nancy A. "Military Outlines New Policy on Gays." *Charlotte Observer*, January 29, 2011, sec. A.

Index

Numbers in **_bold italics_** indicate pages with photographs.